S

MAIN LINE RAILWAYS
AROUND WIGAN

BOB PIXTON

RUNPAST

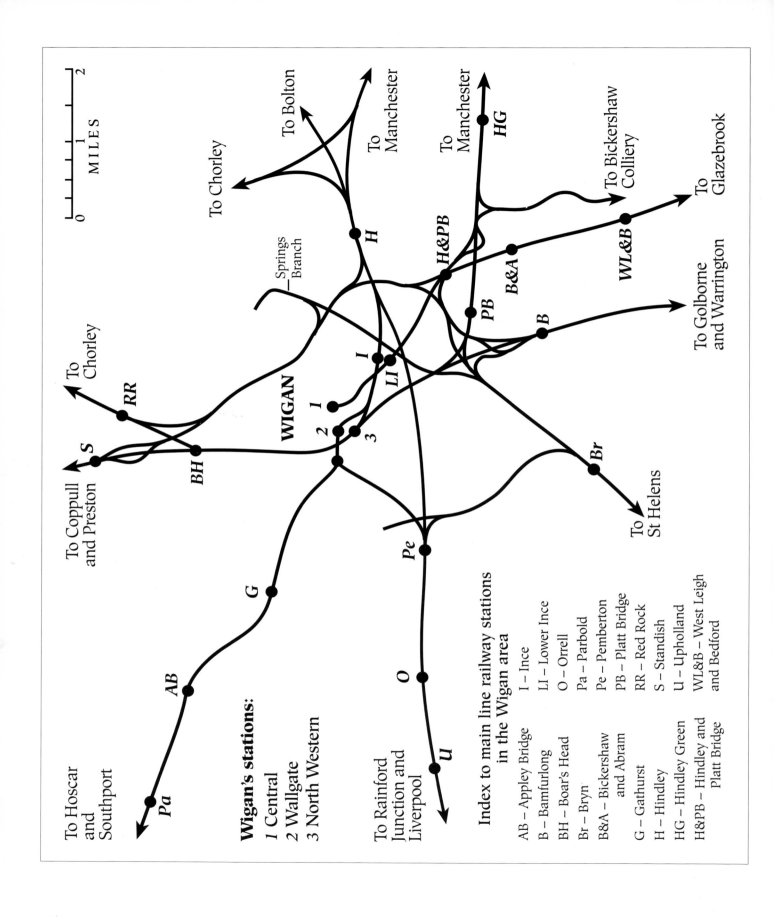

Wigan's stations:
1 Central
2 Wallgate
3 North Western

Index to main line railway stations
in the Wigan area

AB – Appley Bridge
B – Bamfurlong
BH – Boar's Head
Br – Bryn
B&A – Bickershaw
    and Abram
G – Gathurst
H – Hindley
HG – Hindley Green
H&PB – Hindley and
    Platt Bridge

I – Ince
LI – Lower Ince
O – Orrell
Pa – Parbold
Pe – Pemberton
PB – Platt Bridge
RR – Red Rock
S – Standish
U – Upholland
WL&B – West Leigh
    and Bedford

MILES

To Hoscar
and
Southport

To Coppull
and Preston

To Chorley

To Rainford
Junction and
Liverpool

WIGAN

Springs
Branch

To Bolton

To Chorley

To
Manchester

To
Manchester

To Bickershaw
Colliery

To
Glazebrook

To Golborne
and Warrington

To
St Helens

Title page: Wigan – a town built on coal. Bickershaw Colliery in the early years of this century.

J Peden collection

CONTENTS

© 1999 Bob Pixton and Runpast Publishing, Kingscote Grove, Cheltenham, Gloucestershire.

Printed by The Amadeus Press Ltd., Huddersfield.
Typesetting and reproduction by Viners Wood Associates – 01452 812813.

ISBN 1 870754 45 X

Above: The unique 4-6-2 No.71000 *Duke of Gloucester* approaches Wigan North Western station on 28 May 1960 hauling a London to Perth express.

Ray Farrell

Below: Pacific No.46252 *City of Leicester* passes Springs Branch No.1 signal box on 5 May 1962 with an express.

B G Barlow / J Peden collection

INTRODUCTION

This book has its origins in a desire to unravel the complex railway network that existed in the staem era in south Lancashire. The project expanded and was split into titles on the Warrington area, the Widnes/St Helens area – both already published – and this volume.

The railway infrastructure developed around Wigan as it rapidly became a centre for mining activities in the south Lancashire coalfield. One of the first lines from the 'backbone' of the Liverpool & Manchester Railway was to Wigan. Lines north to Preston, west to Southport, Rainford and Liverpool, with its docks, east to Bolton and then Manchester followed soon afterwards. Wigan thus became a railway 'crossroads'.

Transport of goods on the canal system survived the railways' coming, giving customers a choice of carrier, depending on the destination. In fact, coal was last carried by canal to Westwood Power Station in 1972. It wasn't long before the railways were taken over by bigger concerns. This resulted in the east west line becoming part of the L&Y, with the L&NWR running north to south with a branch south-west to St. Helens and the docks at Widnes. Congestion became a big problem with Wigan as the bottleneck, not only in through traffic, but also in handling of wagons, both full and empty. Avoiding lines became the order of the day, the Pemberton loop being the L&Y's southern line bypassing Wigan station, while the L&NWR's was the easterly Whelley loop.

Arriving late in the day was the MS&LR, in the shape of a line from Glazebrook, on the Liverpool-Manchester CLC main line, part of a grand plan to go to Blackpool, but only getting as far as Wigan.

The coalfield here is criss-crossed with faults and the history of the industry is littered, much more than anywhere else, with openings and closures of mines having short lives. As the industry sought to fend off competition from other pits, and abroad, Wigan's ones closed and now there is little such activity and little evidence that there ever was much due to reclamation projects and the great growth in south Lancashire's population.

Whilst the later lines have now been closed, much of the original railway infrastructure is still up and running. High speed electric trains whisk off passengers to London and Glasgow with ease and regularity. The lines west and east are dominated by 'Pacer' and other such multiple units with regular trains to Liverpool via St. Helens, Southport, Bolton and Manchester. By changing trains at Kirkby, passengers can gain access to the Merseyside system and so go right into the centre of the city quite easily.

Long live the train!

Above: Post-war Scottish express. Pacific No.6240 *City of Coventry* hauls at least 15 coaches north at Golborne. Built as a red streamliner in March 1940, the black paint was applied in November 1945. The aerodynamic casing was removed in June 1947.

Chapter One

The London & North Western line north of Wigan to Boar's Head, Standish and Coppull

This line was opened on 31 October 1838 by the North Union Railway, an amalgamation of the Preston & Wigan Railway and Wigan Branch Railway. It was later leased to the Grand Junction Railway and the Manchester & Leeds, before being absorbed by the L&Y/L&NWR on 7 August 1888.

Above: Coppull Station, 1957. Heading north along the down slow is 'Black Five' 4-6-0 No.45437, the train's headlamp code denoting 'Parcels, newspaper, fish, milk, meat, horse and perishables'. The platforms were either side of the slow lines, being connected by a subway. The down line, on the right, was on timber piles being on an embankment: the up side was on firm ground and so had a brick base. The buildings illustrate the modular style that the L&NWR developed, even extending to the canopy and valance in some cases. They were constructed on these lines as a result of the 1888-1895 widening. The connecting subway was also a public right of way. *Stations UK*

Left: Coppull Hall Sidings, 1968. Just under a mile south of Coppull was a set of sidings for local collieries. Access was from the slow lines controlled by this typical L&NWR box of 30 levers. As mines worked out their seams they closed: there was no necessity for this box after 1969. *N.D. Mundy*

Above: Blainscough Sidings, 1965. This box, between Coppull Hall sidings and Coppull station, had 40 levers in a L&NWR tumbler frame and dates from the quadrupling of the lines in 1888-95. It was adjacent to the up main line, not only controlling the four main lines, but also the loops and sidings to the west, accessed from the slow lines. It was swept away by electrification in 1972. *N.D. Mundy*

Below: Coppull, July 1959. On the up fast line is 'Coronation' class No.46243 *City of Lancaster* with a Glasgow to Birmingham express. Until these engines were built by the LMS, Anglo-Scottish trains were hauled by the Fowler 'Royal Scot' class. This necessitated an engine change at Carlisle. Starting life in June 1940, *City of Lancaster* was one of the red streamliners, complete with double chimney. Later it was repainted wartime black in January 1944. The streamlining was in place until April 1948 when it received its BR number. Smoke deflectors were added in 1949 and after blue, green and red liveries it was withdrawn in September 1964 with over 1.5 million miles covered. *RAS/Photomatic*

Left, top: Standish station, circa 1905. From its opening to 1844 it was known as Standish Lane and for over 40 years was a simple rural passing station on the route to Scotland. In 1895 the line north of the junction was quadrupled as far as Euxton near Preston. There the fast lines were to the east with the slow lines to the west. Looking north shows the down platform to the left and the island platform to the right with the junction signal box at its end. The ornate chimneys and the style of the buildings give the appearance of a structure only half built, as if there was something more to be added to the right. The notices illustrate the access from the adjacent road, there were no goods facilities. The stations at Coppull and Balshaw Lane & Euxton were constructed along similar lines. *LNWR Soc. collection*

Left, bottom: Standish station, 1949. In 1869 the Lancashire Union Railway opened the line that passed about half a mile to the east of Standish. This line connected the towns in the north and east of the county with the coal fields around Wigan and to Garston/Widnes docks via St. Helens. The L&NWR built a connection between these two lines, from Standish on the main line to Whelley Junction on the LU line. This allowed north/south bound trains to by-pass the congested Wigan station. At Standish a burrowing junction was built so that down trains from the Whelley line did not cross the main lines on the flat but passed underneath them. The original, 1874, plan was to widen the lines from Bamfurlong, south of Wigan, to Standish and beyond. However, it was 20 years later that part of it (Golborne to Springs Branch in 1888 and Springs Branch to North Western station in 1894, with Standish to Euxton in 1895) was done. The L&NWR

reasoned that the Whelley loop was an additional pair of lines north of Wigan to Standish and so that part remained double, on a rising gradient of 1 in 150. A double-headed excursion on an up express is about to cross Standish Lane bridge. The line it is on continues south to Wigan North Western station. However, the LMS signals indicate that soon it will take the Whelley loop line, off to the east to avoid the station on its way south. *Stations UK*

Above: North of Standish Junction. 1957. An unidentified L&NWR 0-8-0 is passing south on 11 May. It is passing from the slow line onto the fast line, and in a few moments will branch onto the Whelley line. These were some of the few engines that never carried a number on their smoke box. They moved countless tons of coal and empties from collieries to stations and docks before their replacement by the more youthful Stanier '8F's, and the decline in this type of train load. *C.H.A. Townley*

Overleaf, top: South of Standish Junction, 1957. Bringing a long unfitted freight into the station on 11 May is an unidentified L&NWR 0-8-0. It is signalled to go onto the down slow line by signals probably as old as itself. To the right is the connection with the Whelley line. *C.H.A. Townley*

9

Above: Standish Junction, 1967. Taking the main line through the station and on to Wigan, is a Carlisle to Margam freight on the last day of March. Hauling it is Standard class 9F 2-10-0 No.92208 sporting a fitted freight headcode. This meant that at least one third – or in this case it looks like most – of the wagons have continuous brakes: this enabled higher speeds to be scheduled. The 9Fs were no mean achievers in this respect, although they were officially restricted to speeds of less than 60 mph. This example was built at Swindon in 1959-60, and so had a very short working life. The train is leaving the up slow and is crossing the down fast. It will pass Standish station and then take the up Wigan line. If the other signal arm had been pulled off then it would have indicated the Whelley loop line. *Allan Heyes*

Left, bottom: Standish Junction, 1964. 'Britannia' class 4-6-2 No.70039 *Sir Christopher Wren* is hauling an up goods on 27 June along the up slow line. In a short distance the line will curve east to meet the LU line at Whelley Junction. This engine was built at Crewe early in 1953 with a double chimney. Hand rails on the smoke deflectors were removed to aid sighting following an accident at Didcot in 1955. *Ray Farrell*

Overleaf, top: Boars Head. Just a mile south of Standish is Boars Head Junction. This was the joining of the North Union line and the 1869 Lancashire Union line from Blackburn via Chorley. This pre-nationalisation photograph shows it in all its glory. The main station buildings are in the 'V' of the up main and down branch platforms, accessed by a lane from the nearby main road. Next to the buildings was a specially constructed signal box. The platforms were connected by a fine iron footbridge which had connections to local footpaths: its shallow curve fits splendidly into the scene. The bridges necessitated very tall signals with lower repeater arms. The down branch starter post also carries a wrong side up arm to assist sighting. *Author's collection*

Overleaf, bottom: Boars Head Junction signal box, looking north, 1954. Although the station closed on 1 January 1949, the line to Blackburn remained open for many years. This 18 lever box is a typical L&NWR wooden cabin on a steel frame rather than the traditional brick, its height was to assist sighting of both the branch and the main line. The signals are interesting. The main line ones are LMS arms, with the lower post being timber while the branch has a lattice post. Victoria Colliery is in the background. *A.G. Ellis*

11

South of Boars Head, 1954. Just visible under the bridge is the signal box at Boars Head. Hauling an excursion from Blackpool on 19 April is unrebuilt 'Patriot' class 6P5F 4-6-0 No.45543 *Home Guard*. Some 18 members of this class were rebuilt while others were not. This was due to a post-war assessment of the number of 7P engines that the LMS thought necessary – 91 – what precision! After the first 18 such conversions in 1946-9, the programme was stopped due to the imminent appearance of the new BR Standard classes.

A.G. Ellis

Above: Rylands Sidings, 1963. Racing northwards on 13 July is 'Royal Scot' class 4-6-0 No.46118 *Royal Welch Fusilier*. By the mid 1940s, the class was over 15 years old and had frame fractures and smoke-boxes that could not be kept air tight. No.46118 is the 1946 rebuilt type: the class 2A boiler looks similar to its original. The external modifications to the original included the replacement of the flat smoke deflectors with the curved variety, and top feed. Rebuilding gave the engines a new lease of life. *Ray Farrell*

Left: Rylands Sidings signal box, 1969. The sidings here connected to Rylands Mill, which was south and to the east of the line, and to collieries to the north and west which lasted until 1963, the box remaining as a block post until electrification in 1972. In its heyday its 30 levers in a L&NWR frame controlled the extensive loops and sidings to both up and down lines. *M.A. King*

CHAPTER TWO

Wigan's North Western Station

Opening to a terminus at Chapel Lane on 3 September 1832 was the Wigan Branch Railway line. Three trains a day arrived from the Liverpool-Manchester line at Parkside. Shortly afterwards, a line north of Wigan was developed by the Preston and Wigan Railway. However, by the time of opening on 21 October 1838, the two companies had joined forces to become the North Union Railway, in May 1834. The station the NUR opened for the 21,000 population was on the site of today's station.

By the time the town's population doubled, the station was enlarged by the addition of a down loop and a turntable some time before 1880. The gradient north often necessitated banking engines that would be turned there. The opening of a connection between the LU and L&NWR at Standish in the early 1880s led to the routing of many goods and mineral trains that way to avoid the station. An enlarged L&Y goods yard swept away some of the buildings between the footbridge and Wallgate.

Above: Bridge over L&Y line, 1960. Looking north over the roof tops of Wigan sees 'Coronation' class 4-6-2 No.46256 *Sir William A Stanier, F.R.S.* about to enter North Western station on 28 May. This engine was the penultimate of the class when built at Crewe in 1947. One modification, visible in this view, was the flanges on the radial arms of the fabricated one-piece cast trailing truck. This cracked soon after entering service and the last of the class, 46257, was delayed until a new design was produced. While the pair were waiting for new trailing trucks they were fitted with electric lights, the generator being to the rear of the smoke deflectors on the right-hand side. The signal gantry in the 1941 picture has been replaced by colour light with route indicators; left for platform 1 and right for platform 4.   *Ray Farrell*

Right: Bridge over the L&Y, looking south, 1941. The line north passes over the L&Y line to Southport, where signals can be seen on the left of the picture. The photographer is standing on the up main line and the controlling signal gantry stands out clearly. The most important route, the main line through platform 2, has its

arms on the tallest post. To the left the arms were for the up loop, platform 1, while the single arms were for bay platform 5 and the taller one, for the up slow, platform 4.   *British Railways*

15

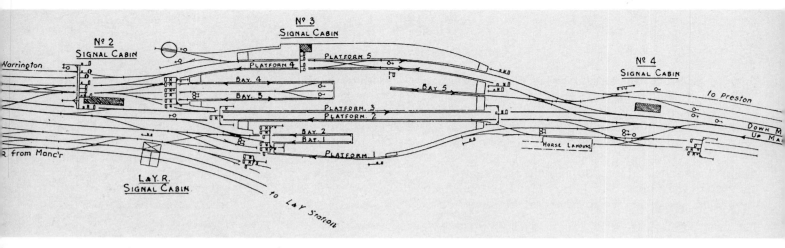

Above: Map of Wigan North Western station, pre 1941.

Below: Map of 1847.

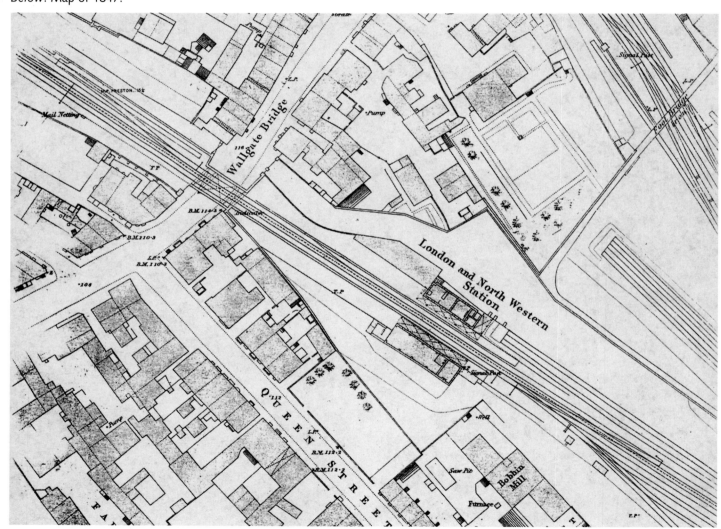

Above: No.2 box. This view, taken from a northbound train in 1967, shows the flat roof and 'modern' appearence well. The box controlled movements at the northern end of the station. It replaced No.4 box which was unusual in being of wooden construction: others in the area were typical L&NWR tall brick structures. There was a 112 lever frame, only 71 were used: perhaps the engineers thought that the lines north were to be quadrupled one day and so were prepared. *M. Christensen*

Left: View south from No.2 box, 1960. Leaving platform 3 on 28 May is 'Jubilee' class 4-6-0 No.45625 *Sarawak* on a down excursion. The main lines show up clearly as do the up/down slow lines, platforms 4 and 5, each with an engine on. The northern bay, No.5, can also be seen together with the the roof covering platforms 3 and 4. This engine was one of the Crewe built batch (10/1934) that had a slightly shorter wheel base, and with a 3″ shorter bogie, compatible with the 'Patriots', but not with hundreds of Class Five 4-6-0s and Class Four 2-6-4Ts. When new it was attached to a 3,500 gallons, 5.5 tons of coal tender, but with higher sides and curving top edge making it indistinguishable from the higher capacity Stanier types. *Ray Farrell*

Overleaf, bottom: View north from No.2 box, 1960. Steaming into the station is 'Coronation' class 4-6-2 No.46235 *City of Birmingham* on 28 May with a very long southbound express. This shows nicely the curve into the station and the relatively simple layout – up/down lines with carriage sidings on both sides. Only two lines were ever built between Wigan and Standish Junction, some 3 miles north. *Ray Farrell*

Left, top: Down side bays, 1941. There were two such bays between platforms 3 and 4 at the southern end of the station. These provided finishing places for local services from Liverpool, Manchester and Warrington. Engine release crossovers were connected to a central track on which the photographer was standing. This fine L&NWR gantry with short arms controlled movements from the bays. Two choices were possible to trains after they had gone past the signal box – to the left and the up main or right, onto the up slow line. All three lines have small 'calling on' arms to assist with shunting. The dominating building in the middle of the lines is Wigan No.2. a massive L&NWR style box with 148 levers. Its height, at least 10' taller than normal boxes, was to enable it to get sufficient sight of the movements it was controlling. Beyond the box is the inner home gantry controlling down movements, the main line signals, on the left, are hidden by the box while the other arms are for routes from slow to main, the bays and down relief, platform 5. To the left a 'Lanky' 0-6-0 engine is shunting in the goods yard. The abutments are for the bridge over Chapel Lane. *British Railways*

Below: Platform 4, 1960. L&NER class 'J10' 0-6-0 No.65192 is seen working away from its home shed of Warrington (Dallam), 8B. The loco is on the old platform 4 line which was signalled for bi-directional use. Down trains could arrive or up trains could depart from it. Just visible on the curve is the scissors crossover making it effectively two platforms in one. Controlling these, almost avoiding lines, and the turntable at the southern end, was No.5 box up on a gantry. Before 1924 the sign would have simply said 'Wigan'. The frame work for the canopies, with a smoke trough, is well illustrated. The bay behind the loco., bay 5, was built for the Blackburn trains (north via Boar's Head) to depart. Blackburn could also be reached from the L&Y station, east via Hindley then north and Blackrod, with both lines meeting at Chorley. *Ray Farrell*

Above: Down lines, 1941. The northern ends of the platforms are on top of the Wallgate street overbridge – hence the notice next to the L&NWR water column at the end of platform 3, the down main. Oddly enough there appears not to be a notice at the end of platform 5, on the left, which is where mineral trains would have waited for faster passenger trains, and so more likely to have used the facility. The signal gantry is necessary as the main line is on a curve and to enable engine drivers to see them at a reasonable distance away they were actually on the right hand of the running track. All of the signal posts have two arms on them. The bottom distant signal is controlled by the box in front – Wigan No.4 – and the upper stop signal by the box of that section, namely Wigan No.2 some three hundred yards south. Also on the same gantry is a small 'calling on' arm, most often used for shunting purposes. In the distance can be seen box No.4 and just behind is its 1941 ARP replacement, destined to become Wigan No.2. *British Railways*

Above: Up main line, 1959. Travelling south is an Edinburgh to Birmingham express hauled by 'Princess' class 4-6-2 No.46200 *The Princess Royal* on 21 September. Around this time these engines were having a chequered career. The entire class was mothballed at one stage due to an excess of motive power, when new diesels became available, only to be bought back into service later. Six locos were returned for traffic in January 1962, being finally withdrawn the following Autumn, this one in November 1962. The bay platforms were built so that passengers could change trains with the minimum of movement. So, passengers from up trains had to walk a few yards to bays 1 and 2 for up stopping trains to Warrington, Manchester or St. Helens. Likewise for the down trains, passengers arriving at bays 4 and 5 had a short walk for their down train, usually at platforms 3 or 4. In this way movement around the station, with ample opportunity to end up in the wrong place, was reduced. An unidentified 'Black 5' waits by the water column on platform 1 while, hiding in bay 3, which had been renumbered platform 5, is a Derby 2-car multiple unit on the Liverpool, St. Helens to Wigan service. When these were introduced on this route in January 1959 there was a vast increase in passengers, mainly due to the regularity of the service, almost doubled. It is estimated that two years later the number of passengers had more than trebled compared with steam days.   *Ray Farrell*

Right, top: Up side bays, 1941. In between the up island platforms 1 and 2, were bays 1 and 2, complete with massive hydraulic buffer stops – they are still there today. Both joined at a double slip crossing allowing movements onto the lines for Manchester (L&Y lines adjacent), to Liverpool (up loop) or to Warrington (up fast).

Oddly, the signals controlling the routes from platform 1 have longer arms: most of the distant (lower) arms are 'fixed' telling the driver that he should expect the next stop signal to be 'on' and so he should keep his speed low and be ready to stop. Partially hidden by the hoist is the up main home signal – pulled off – almost on its own gantry for sighting purposes. Dissimilar are the companies' watering facilities, the L&Y preferring a Horwich parachute tank to the L&NWR's platform mounted ones. The L&Y signal box, their No.1, was astride their running lines where a very short trip working is being taken by an 0-6-0 loco., No.1, and the mighty L&NWR No.2 box, were combined together in the ARP Wigan No.1 from 1941. This was about half a mile south where the Manchester lines diverged from the Warrington lines. Some interesting platform paraphernalia is on view, ranging from gas lamps, with metal notices, luggage trolley and a hoist at the end of platform 2. This connected to one at the end of platform 3 and was used for the transfer of perishables e.g fish, milk and market produce.

British Railways

Right, bottom: Changing motive power at Wigan. Around 50 years separate the next three views, taken from practically the same place. In 1914 'Cauliflower' 0-6-0 No.539 waits at the up main platform with a local train. The gantry over the up bays shows up nicely. Facilities then, in the station's heyday, would have been very different than in later days. Separate rooms existed for 1st and 3rd classes, males and females, toilets, refreshment and waiting rooms. The station master had more than 75 people working under him, including clerks, police, shunters and station staff.

R.S. Carpenter collection

Above: In 1954 'Royal Scot' class 4-6-0 No.46114 *Coldstream Guardsman* is putting up plenty of smoke from its double chimney as it passes south.

Photomatic

Below: In 1962 English Electric Type 4 No.D227 is pulling a similar train. In 15 years time the scene would change again to today's one of overhead wires and electric locos.

Norman Preedy

Above: Up main platform, circa 1955. On what most people think of as a typical Lancashire day, the young trainspotters in short trousers, gabardine coats and school caps discuss the merits of 'Crab' 2-6-0 No.42719 waiting at the up main platform with an excursion. Shed 27D was Bury. Ready to depart from the up bay is Stanier 2-6-4T No.42462, probably for Manchester. The footbridge across the Top goods yard, complete with crane, can be seen on the right. *N Stead collection*

Below: North Western Station, 1964. Photographs of old platform 5, on the right, are rare because it was used for few trains and then mostly excursions or north-bound freights. At 265 yards it was the shortest platform, with two short sidings and a turntable for banking engines at its southern end. 'Black Five' No.45083 is in the bi-directional platform 9 on 28 August. It is interesting to note that the station signs only give the town, whereas the large nameboards give the station its full title. *A.G. Ellis*

Above: Wigan L&NWR goods yard, looking north. Although there were a large number of freight trains in the area, the goods yard may seem 'modest'. It must be remembered that there were several coal yards in the town and that each of the three railway companies had their own goods yard in the town. The L&NWR goods yard was to the south of the station and Chapel Lane. Over time the facilities expanded until there were three sheds, one of which is seen here in this view to the north. To the right are the main running lines. Apart from the covered sheds for unloading and storage, there were three long sidings. The surrounding areas were made up to the top of the rail level with stone setts. In this way carts could be moved around the yard easily without damaging them. Although still in use in 1957, the wide layout of the yard would have been used to its full potential in the first and second decades of this century with the whole area bustling with crates, sacks, boxes and animals being loaded/unloaded and stacked ready for movement. Two sets of posts with electric lamps were put up in the 1940s so that early morning/late evening work could be carried out: the concrete surrounds are necessary to protect the posts from traffic accidents. With today's massive lorries even this protection wouldn't be sufficient.

The transfer from rail to road was done in the 1950s using articulated vehicles nicknamed 'mechanical horses'. The three wheeled motor units were very manouverable – an essential quality in the narrow confines of most goods yards built for the horse and cart era. Trailers, several of which can be seen with various loads, were quite short and could only carry small loads, in comparison to today's 38 tonne monsters. *British Railways*

Right, top: Wigan No.1 signal box exterior, 1971. The 1941 replacement of semaphore signals and boxes led to the building of three ARP boxes in the Wigan area – Wigan No.1, Wigan No. 2 (shown earlier in this chapter) and Wigan Wallgate (pictured in chapter eight). The LMS specifications were for 14" solid brick walls, a 12" thick reinforced-concrete flat roof, and no locking room windows, all designed to keep vital structures as damage proof as possible. Strangely enough for the time, its name was made up of concrete panels. The name, but not the number, was quickly covered up for the duration of the war. This box replaced Ince Hall box, on the ex-L&Y line, Wallgate No.1 and the ex-L&NWR Nos. 1, 2 and 3 boxes, with eight men doing the work previously done by 20. There were two frames. 85 levers were in the western one while the central frame had 40 levers in it. While this box went with the electrification scheme in the 1970s others in different parts of the country stand derelict due to demolition problems, testimony to the design specifications! This box was situated with the Warrington lines in front and the Manchester lines behind, their gradients necessitate the use of catch points. To the right of the box is a subway and behind it is part of the gas works. *M. Christensen*

Right, bottom: Wigan No.1 signal box interior, 1960. No.1 box controlled all the southern approaches to both Wallgate and North Western stations. Simplifications include removal of old bay 5 (platform 9), engine releases from bays 3 and 4, and the exit from platform 1 and the up loops. The colour lights and the slimline box did much to relieve the visual 'clutter' of the station.

Adrian Vaughan collection

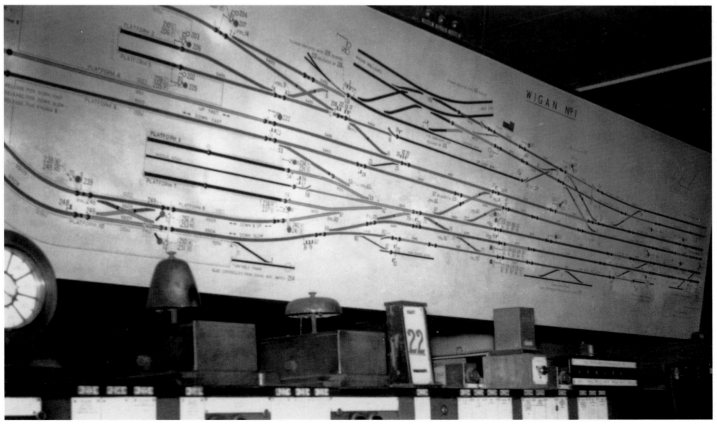

Top: Southern approach to Wigan North Western, 1940. The photographer was standing in the up main line looking south. The abutments on the left are for the bridge over the canal and behind the middle signal post is Wigan No.1 box. In the background is Westwood Lane bridge with James, Fredrick and William Street on the left. For several miles south of Wigan the line allows fast running as it is has little gradient or curve. The six tracks may seem rather excessive. The fast lines are the middle pair with their next major set of points being at Manchester Junction, some 2 miles distant. The slow lines are to the east and at a similar distance they will meet the line to St. Helens at Liverpool Junction. The left hand pair of lines went to Springs Branch Junction where the main loco. shed was situated. *Author's collection*

Above: South of Wigan, 1961. Two days before Christmas sees Stanier class 4 2-6-4T No.42612 coming around the ex-L&Y curve by the gas works to be at the same level as the ex-L&NWR lines. This engine was one of a very successful class of 625. However, this overall number hides the three different designers – Fowler, Stanier and Fairburn; two types of boiler – parallel and taper; and wheelbases. They were very successful at doing this type of job – suburban passenger services. On the extreme right is box No.1.

A.K. Jones collection

CHAPTER THREE

The London & North Western line south of Wigan to Golborne and Bamfurlong

Golborne Junction came into existence in 1864 when the L&NWR made a direct line for their Wigan-Warrington trains. Previous to this, they had to pass by way of the triangles at Earlestown and Parkside, with a short trip along the Liverpool-Manchester main line. The new line, just over 2 miles long, left the line to Earlestown at Winwick Junction and then burrowed under the L&M main line before rejoining the 1832 ex-NUR line at Golborne Junction. Between 1888 and 1894 the L&NWR quadrupled the line from Golborne and Wigan.

Above: Golborne Junction, 28 July 1962. An up fitted freight hauled by 'Black Five' 4-6-0 No.45072 passes on the Winwick lines, with the Lowton ones on the right. Sidings at Newton-le-Willows allowed slower moving freight trains to make way so that faster passenger trains on the main line could overtake them. The rather tall signal box, which illustrates the sighting problems in the area, survived from the quadrupling of the line, until electrification in 1973. A double set of windows was provided as the locking room was about four foot taller than normal, again illustrating the sighting problems there. It is a 'type 4' box with the barge board set directly over the boarding and finials inserted into the boarding. The middle panes of glass were fixed and, to enable cleaning, a walk way was provided. *A.K. Jones Collection*

Left, above: Between Golborne Junction and station, 1961. 'Coronation' class 4-6-2 No.46242 *City of Glasgow*, two months short of its 21st birthday, is racing along the up fast line approaching the junction on 23 March. When built at Crewe it had the famous red streamlining and a double chimney. Streamlining wasn't an engineering success and it was removed in March 1947 being rebuilt along conventional lines, but with some streamlining features retained, such as the chamfering at the top of the smokebox door. This loco. was involved in the famous Harrow collision with 'Jubilee' No.45637 *Windward Islands* in October 1952. The 'Jubilee' was scrapped soon after while this engine was rebuilt; a circular smoke box door was put in which lasted until withdrawn in 1963, the loco. having covered one and a half million miles.   *J.A. Peden*

Left, below: Golborne station, looking north. This, and nearby Bamfurlong, were a pair of outwardly similar stations, this one was opened by the North Union Railway around 1839 to serve nearby collieries. The bridge over the line superseded a level crossing there called 'Golborne Gates'. A two-storey platform level building served as a booking hall and entrance from the adjacent road. Steps led down to both platforms where there were brick-built passenger facilities. The platform mounted box controlled the slow lines, denoted by the circle on the signal's arm, and the entrance to the colliery in the west. The fast lines are to the right, they had no platform connections, and their own 26 lever signal box which closed with electrification. *Bernard Matthews collection*

Above: North of Golborne station 1961. Looking north towards Wigan sees an up Workington to Euston excursion on 16 June, hauled by 'Royal Scot' class 4-6-0 No.46148 *The Manchester Regiment*. The engine was rebuilt in July 1954 after being in service for almost 25 years. The most visible changes were the double chimney and curved smoke deflectors. Here it is seen running in the livery of dark green lined with orange and black, a 1957 BR crest is on the tender. The bridge in the background carries the 1895 line from Lowton St. Mary to St. Helens. That line's station, of the same name as the L&NWR's, meant name changes when they both became part of British Railways after nationalisation. The former became the 'North' station and the latter became the 'South' station.   *I.G. Holt*

Above: Edge Green & Golborne Colliery Sidings box. The busiest part of the ex-GC system was the eastern part between Lowton St. Mary's and this signal box. It served the branch to Crompton's sidings, off to the right and Golborne Colliery, off to the left. The latter was worked by propelling empty wagons, as this 4F 0-6-0 No.44490 has done in March 1961. Full wagons left the colliery onto the ex-L&NWR main line. In 1968 a spur was built to join the two previously separate lines, L&NWR and GC, north of the bridge at Golborne. At various times this has served local industries, Lowton Metals and Haydock Colliery, and more lately, the tarmacadam roadstone plant on the site of Edge Green colliery, with tankers from Immingham bringing raw materials.   *Eddie Bellass*

Above: Bamfurlong Junction, 1952. In 1882 the L&NWR opened up lines from Whelley, on the LU line, to their main line at Standish. This, and the absorption of the LU line, were operational responses to the situation at the time. The large number of collieries, each with their connections, often to more than one line, meant that the control of operations was slow and, in a competitive age, something had to be done. In an attempt to rationalise and control the situation the L&NWR decided to make a series of sorting sidings to the east of the main line, north of Bamfurlong's overbridge over the Leigh Branch of the Leeds-Liverpool canal. Such sidings needed to not only be appropriately situated to reduce costs, but also to have sufficient connections for incoming and outgoing traffic. The connections and improvements took place in three phases. Firstly, in 1886 the Platt Bridge Junction Railway was built to allow direct south to east running from the L&NWR to the LU lines. Incidentally, the connection on the Wigan Junction Railway to the Eccles to Wigan line opened at the same time and so allowed movement in the Manchester direction to and from collieries in the Plank and Bickershaw areas. In 1888 there was a major rebuilding of the lines south of Wigan. The former LU line, and the connection at Standish, were increasingly being used as a bypass for the congested Wigan station (to be rebuilt in 1894) and to avoid the northbound gradient of two miles of 1 in 150 from the station. To get the mineral trains from the sorting sidings on to the Platt Bridge line, the latter was made to dive under the main line to

emerge on the east by the sidings. Connections from the former LU line also assisted operations – from the St. Helens direction to the sorting sidings, extra sidings on the St. Helens-Wigan curve and from on top of the L&NWR line down to the Manchester line from Fir Tree Junction. This 1952 view is between the four main lines, the fast to the right and the slow to the left, the signal box is Bamfurlong Junction. Immediately north of the bridge is a pair of lines branching from the slow lines, these will serve the sorting sidings with the line for the burrowing junction coming off a little beyond them. The up line can be seen joining the fast line just the other side of the bridge. The photographer was standing next to the fast-slow connections: in this way goods/passenger trains could use the Whelley loop to avoid Wigan station.

British Railways

Left: Bamfurlong Station. The station was, like Golborne, accessed from an adjacent overbridge, Lilly Lane, but here it led to wooden platform facilities as this view north shows. Opened by the Wigan Branch Railway on 3 September 1832, it was closed by British Railways in 1950. The fast lines are to the right and had no platforms servicing them. Under the bridge wagons can be seen in the sorting sidings while on the left is the connection to Bamfurlong Colliery. Like many collieries it was also connected to the adjacent canal. While it is fashionable to suppose that canals gave way to rail, many collieries sent coal by both methods depending upon the destination and ease of transfer. *Stations UK*

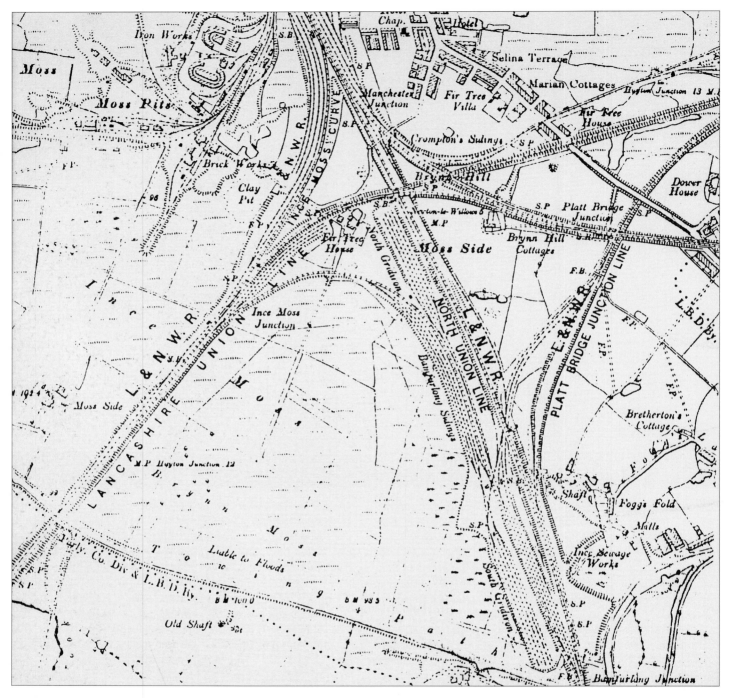

Above: Bamfurlong Sorting Sidings. These were built to the west of the main line and consisted of two sets of 12 dead end sidings feeding a series of loops. As the ground was basically flat then shunting engines were used, typically 0-6-0T, 0-8-2T as well as 0-8-0 and 0-6-0 tender engines from Springs Branch loco. depot. The method of operation was for a train to arrive at the loops from collieries and other towns. The wagons would be shunted into the dead end sidings where trains were assembled. By means of reversal, it was possible for trains to go from either sidings grid to almost any point of the compass. In 1891, 20 trains per day were booked over the former LU line to Garston's docks using the extra sidings at Ince Moss Junction for holding: the widening of the line to St. Helens was a welcome relief.

Right, above: Bamfurlong Sorting Sidings signal box. In front of the 64 lever L&NWR tumbler frame box are the up/down goods lines. These left the slow main lines at Bamfurlong Junction and will soon swing east to pass under the main lines that the photo was taken from. Once under the quadruple main lines, they will branch into the east goods (to pass up by Springs Branch), or continue to Platt Bridge Junction. *M.A. King*

Right, below: Bamfurlong Sorting Sidings, 1952. Having just brought a train of coal wagons onto the sidings, the engine awaits its next turn. By this time, members of Aspinall's Class 27 built from 1889 were feeling their age! *Brian Hoper collection*

Above: Main line at Springs Branch. 8F 2-8-0 No 48675 has just joined the West Coast main line at Springs Branch with a loaded coal train from Abram to Ribble Sidings on 8 May 1967.

Allan Heyes

Left, above: Main line at Springs Branch. Heading a down express in 1933 is one of Whale's 19" Goods passing the loco. shed. By this time it was in LMS livery and numbering. Unfortunately the smoke obscures the wonderful L&NWR signals.   *H.F. Wheller*

Left, below: Main line at Springs Branch. 3 September 1966, sees 9F No.92033 passing Box No.1 with a southbound freight train. It is passing along the goods only lines. The route signalled above the engine is interesting. The pair of tracks pass under the main lines to come up on the west leading to Bamfurlong sorting sidings. A branch comes off from them to pass east towards Manchester: this is the route set. However, the line ahead is occupied and so the signal is on. The small, lower calling on arm is off allowing the driver to proceed with caution along the line to the next stop signal. This was a device whereby a train could be sent forward from one section to increase track capacity, without it being accepted by the section in front. An 8F is by the coaling stage.   *Ray Farrell*

Right: Map of the LNWR main line in the Wigan vicinity.

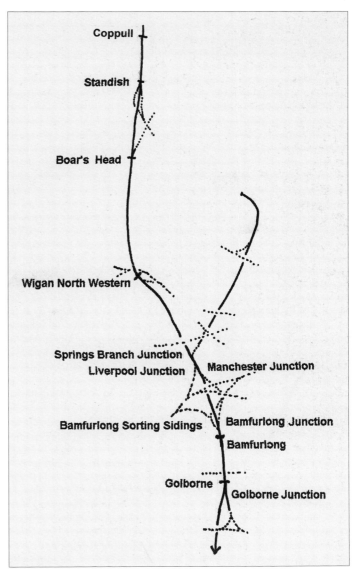

35

Left: Springs Branch No.1, interior, 1956. The 80 lever frame faces the windows which look out onto the lines the box controls. In the middle of the box is the line diagram, which from the days of track circuiting will have small light bulbs on it which will show occupancy of the track. On either side of the diagram, are the dials that show if the line is clear or occupied. The levers take some pulling, hence the stirrup. Behind each lever is a brass plate that describes the lever.

Signalling Record Society, Scrimgeour collection

Below: Springs Branch No.1 signal box, 1969. This view was taken from a moving train and shows the box just before its demise and takeover by Warrington's new box in 1972. The southernmost box is No.1 with its brick base and wooden cabin. The entrance was at the back. The steps were at the other end. Initially, the L&NWR had its signal boxes contracted out to Saxby & Farmer. Due to the expense the company decided from 1872 to begin 'in-house' manufacture of signalling equipment at Crewe, it would take many years before they did all their own. This box embodies the principle construction format: brick base and a timber frame on top, although there were exceptions to the former as conditions dictated – No.2 box was completely wooden in its construction which usually signified unstable ground. Even the bricks were made by the company and the timber frames were built to a standard design.

M.A. King

Left: Springs Branch, 1966. Waiting at the down slow signals, controlled by No.2 box, is an 8F on 1 September.   *Ray Farrell*

Below: Westwood Power Station. This was developed on land to the west of the main line, next to where the canal passes under it and the canal's Leigh branch joins it. The land was previously used as an athletic grounds. Commissioned in 1951, it was two years before coal sidings were built and used from 1954-1962. The adjacent canal provided the coal in the early days from Bickershaw Colliery and in the last years of its operations. The last barges arrived in 1972, then coal came by road. After being 'in reserve' for many years following closure in the early 1980s the whole lot was blown up and demolished in 1989. 24 June 1961 sees 'Royal Scot' class 4-6-0 No.46126 passing the power station with an up excursion. Estate agents describing houses in Westwood Terrace had their work cut out as they were surrounded by the main line and associated coal sidings, canal and the power station.

Ray Farrell

Manchester Junction, 1967. 'Britannia' class Pacific No.70013 *Oliver Cromwell* is leaving Wigan with the combined 11.50 ex-Blackpool and the 11.00 ex-Windermere, to Euston on 24 July. The engine was built at Crewe just over 16 years earlier and carries the second, 1957, BR emblem, the lion holding the wheel. (The first, mid 1948, was the lion astride the wheel). Originally, this was handed, i.e. in two forms so that the lion always faced towards the front no matter which side it was on. However, only one version had been approved by the College of Heralds. So, from 1959 only the lion facing left was authorised, on the side we cannot see it is facing backwards!   *J.H. Cooper-Smith*

CHAPTER FOUR

The Springs Branch and its Engine Shed

Before it was opened by the North Union Railway on October 31st 1834, coal was transported by canal. The Leeds-Liverpool canal had been ferrying coal from the Wigan basin to Liverpool from around 1760. Connecting the north of Wigan to Preston was the Lancaster Canal from 1803. The two were joined at Top Lock in 1816 and several branches were built to take the canal closer to the customer e.g. Ince Hall and Leigh branches, the latter joining up to Manchester from 1820. Springs Branch left the NUR main line south of Wigan and roughly paralleled the canal, linking up with collieries, mills and coke works in the east and north of Wigan, even doing the right angled turn near its end, just like the canal. Trade was so brisk that the single line was doubled as far as the Manchester Road from 1845 and to the Haigh saw mills not long after. Some colliery owners were allowed to run their own trains over the railway companies lines until, in June 1854, a Kirkless Hall Colliery coal train was in collision at Springs Branch Junction with a LNWR train for London.

The branch had four overlapping phases. Initially there were numerous colliery connections, many of these changed ownership many times. The line passed through Ince, probably the most productive of the Lancashire coal fields in the Victorian era; many of the collieries were simply called 'Ince Hall' which makes research confusing.

On the back of this came the need to build and repair the large number (estimated between 8-12,000) of private owners wagons so a number of wagon workshops came to prominence around the branch. Overlapping these two themes was the development of the iron/steel industry in the region with by far the largest being Kirkless Iron works towards the northern part of the line.

Finally, the closure of the collieries, iron works and the decline in the wagon repair workshops has led to the total obliteration of the line and the industries with their replacement by derelict land, light industrial units and warehouses.

Some pieces of land have had many uses at different times: that latterly occupied by Central Wagon Works approximately a mile from the junction is a good example. It was opened up by Ince Hall Coal and Canal Co. as a colliery which was taken over by the Chorley Wagon Co. in the early years of this century. In 1911 the Central Wagon Co took over the business: they had other units at Preston, Warrington and Doncaster They expanded the works to both sides of the line after WW1. With the line's primary concern declining, the northern part, from Kirkless workshops to New Springs, was closed in 1932, the remainder singled in 1943.

Central Wagon Works, 1965. During the 1960s the company must have rivalled the Barry scrapyards for the dismantling of steam engines. When this dried up the line from their premises was closed in the late 1970s/early 1980s with the line only extending just under the Warrington road overbridge now.

Below: Not only local engines were cut up, as ex-GWR 'Hall' class 4-6-0 No.4976 *Warfield Hall* sits in the clutter and debris of the cutting yard. *R. Farrell*

Above: How ironic that the demise of steam locos. should breath new life into a declining area. This newly constructed shelter was to enable all-weather work to continue as much as possible. A line of ex-L&NER class B1s wait their turn at the torch, as seen from a passing train. Light industrial units occupy the area now.

R. Farrell

Previous page: Belle Green Crossing, 1956. This view is looking north at a Wigan that has gone forever; the cobbled street, gas lights and not a motor vehicle in sight! To the rear of the photographer there was a branch off to Rose Bridge colliery hence the antique signal post having two arms: the upper stop arm for the level crossing and the lower arm for the forthcoming junction. The signal box appears to be of L&NWR design, dating from when the road was busy enough to need protection, probably around 1870/80. The gates and track are in a dilapidated state. In 1958 the part from Belle Green Lane to Kirkless Hall Junction was closed. In order to get access to the Flag and Tarmacadam works the branch from the former LU line at Rose Bridge Junction was reopened – this lasting until summer 1965. *British Railways*

Above: Manchester Road Crossing, 1956. Progress has arrived in Wigan in the shape of concrete lamp posts and a smattering of motor vehicles but no TV aerials yet. Central Wagon Works was on the left. The signal box was to the north of the crossing and had been disused for some years, but looked in better shape than at Belle Green, a short distance up the line.   *British Railways*

Below: Ince Hall Colliery crossing, 1952. Springs Branch is the double track passing from right to left. Under the bridge is the Central Wagon Works. On the L&Y line a local train, hauled by a 2-6-4T engine, is slowing down in order that it can stop at Ince Station. Protecting the crossing of the line to Low Hall Colliery from Ince Station is what appears to be an original L&NWR signal, with a rather burnt out hut with a lever frame in front of it.   *J. Peden collection*

The L&NWR Loco. Depot at Springs Branch. Originally the company's (and its constituents) loco. sheds were by the goods sheds until 1859 when they became so overcrowded that they were demolished and a two road brick shed opened to the east of the main line; this was followed by an adjacent wooden shed in 1864.

Growth of traffic soon rendered these sheds too small and so in 1869 they made way for an eight road brick shed – No.1. Even by this tlme, smoke chimneys had been removed due to corrosion. As this map extract shows, this too wasn't big enough and so in 1882 another shed of similar size was added – No.2 building.

Bernard Matthews collection

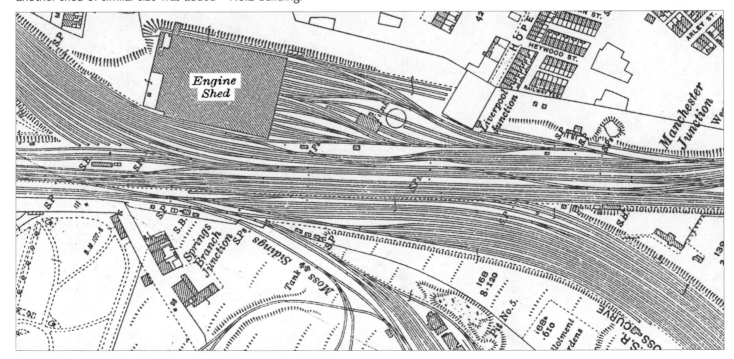

Above: L&NWR 'Cauliflower' loco, circa 1948. The emissions from locos. took their toll of No. 2 shed's roof which was replaced in 1955.

A.K. Jones collection

Below: The decline in the rail system allowed the shed to be reduced to four roads as this early 1960s view shows. By 1965 No. 2 shed had been demolished and the whole site closed to steam in 1967.

Ray Farrell

Steam loco. sheds catered for the daily needs of the engines, minor maintainance and for storage between duties. The following photographs show the shed's daily routines.

Above: Coaling. Moving up in turn on 28 May 1963, are Stanier 8Fs 2-8-0 Nos.48318 and 48631. This style of coaler emptied wagons into a hopper which was tipped into an engine's tender. *P. Hutchinson*

Below: Ash removal. Stanier 2-6-4T No.42462 had been performing this act for nearly thirty years when this 1965 photo was taken. The ash was dropped down in-between the track and then it was shovelled into scoops that were hauled up the tower to the left of the engine to be tipped into adjacent wagons. By this time No.2 building had been demolished. *P. Hutchinson*

Above: Water. A spick and span 'Black 5' 4-6-0 No. 44935 fills its 4,000 gallon tender from a B.R. style water column in 1963. It had three more of its 21 year life left. *P. Hutchinson*

Right: Storage. In its heyday the sixteen roads could only accommodate a fraction of the shed's allocation with the rest having to stand out in the open, much to the delight of passing enthusiasts. Here ex-L&NWR class G2a (locally called 'Fat Nancies') 0-8-0 No. 9136 is under cover on 24 April 1938. *L. Hanson*

Below: Following the closure of Lower Ince shed in 1952, locos. on the former GCR line to Wigan Central that needed servicing went to Springs Branch. L&NER class 02 2-8-0 No.63966 is on shed in 1964. *A.K. Jones*

Chapter Five

The London & North Western line to Platt Bridge and Hindley Green

Manchester Junction, looking south. South of Wigan and adjacent to the Springs Branch loco. shed is the junction of the L&NWR's 'Eccles, Tyldesley and Wigan' line opened on 1 September 1864. On 24 June 1961, Stanier 'Black 5' 4-6-0 No.45109 brings a train onto the main line from Manchester. It has just passed over the pair of freight lines that run south under the bridge on a falling gradient on their way to Bamfurlong sorting sidings. While the Manchester line has four tracks, high speed running wasn't possible as there was a 25mph speed limit in force.

Ray Farrell

Above: Manchester Junction, 1968. Crossing over from the up fast line to the Manchester line is a train of coal empties for Bickershaw Colliery. Putting up a good smoke screen is Stanier 8F 2-8-0 No.48348 on 2 February. The driver appreciates that his train is blocking the main line and so tries to make all due speed across the lines. Hidden by the smoke is the engine shed. The signal box is Springs Branch No.1, while just visible across the sidings is the smaller North Sidings Box. Westwood Power Station is the ghost in the background. *Allan Heyes*

Left: Manchester Junction, looking north. A person standing on Taylor Lane bridge would have this view, on 5 May 1962, of ex-L&NWR class G2a 0-8-0 No.49381 going light engine along the branch. The four tracks are noticeable, the junction being controlled by Springs Branch Junction No.1 signal box. on the western side of the running lines. The loco. depot in the background is Springs Branch, with the coaling plant on the right. *C. Hawkins*

Right: Platt Bridge Junction signal box, 1970. Passing easterly, the Manchester line went underneath the ex-LU line and the four tracks from Springs Branch Junction converged to two. A short distance further on a spur down from the LU's Fir Tree House Junction came to meet the Manchester line: 15mph speed limits restricted movements. This is the view from the Whelley loop lines, east of the 55 lever box. Unusually, the box has a brick base. It was typical L&NWR practice, in areas of subsidence, to make the whole box of wood. The signal box here was unusual in that it not only controlled these junctions, but also the line and junction which passed underneath. It closed in 1973. *M.A. King*

Crompton's Sidings, 1967. Just under the bridge was the connection known as Crompton's Sidings. At various times this has served collieries, wagon works and coke washing plants. It also connected to Fir Tree Sidings which were developed to the east of the Warrington Road. The level crossing across it was removed in 1962, a short while after the last of the businesses there disappeared. Being given the green light to proceed onto the down main line is a train load of coal. Stanier 8F No.48267 hauls the train while sister engine No.48556 has had lever no.14 pulled to allow it to proceed into the engine shed, just under Taylor Lane bridge where the photographer was stood. Platt Bridge Glass Works makes up the background. *Allan Heyes*

Above: Platt Bridge Station. At almost two miles from Wigan, this station is to the west, and accessed from, the Liverpool Road. It has typically wooden L&NWR buildings and platforms as this 1950s view towards Wigan shows. Half a mile east was the ex-WJR/GCR Hindley & Platt Bridge Station. *Stations U.K.*

Below: Bickershaw Junction, June 1960. Going east there were a lot of junctions over the next mile. Connections were put in – east to Scowcroft sidings, west to Platt Bridge junction, south to Abram North and north to Hindley & Platt Bridge Junction – by the L&NWR to connect their Bickershaw line with the WJR's Strangeways Junction. Subsequently, the LU line was accessed by east/west connections at Amberswood. Also from the Manchester line a triangular junction was created by the West Leigh Branch which went south to Plank Lane and Bickershaw Colliery. Passing west from the branch onto the main line is an unidentified LNWR G2a class 0-8-0 engine with a load of coal. *Author's collection*

Left, top: Hindley Green Station. At four miles from Wigan this 1950s view is looking east towards Howe Bridge and shows the standard L&NWR wooden buildings with ramps down from the main road. Even though the line looks straight on the map, it wasn't a very fast line. Fast trains in the early 1950s, including the Eccles stop, made the seventeen and a half mile journey from Wigan to Manchester in 34-38 minutes, with stopping trains taking in excess of 50 minutes. As time went on the problems of subsidence became worse with large amounts of recovery time necessary to keep the trains on time. Although not unaffected, the former L&Y line via Hindley, with its Bolton permutation, was retained and the L&NWR closed on May 1 1961 to passengers.

Stations U.K.

Left, bottom: Abram North. Just over a mile from Bickershaw Junction was a set of exchange sidings with up/down through sidings. NCB loco hauled trains would arrive here from the colliery and leave the wagons. Waiting on the down main line is a BR engine, Stanier 8F 2-8-0 No.48356, complete with brake van. In the background are its wagons. It will cross over to the up line and leave the brake van, regain the down line and pass beyond the wagons. The engine will then push the wagons back to meet the brake van and will cross back onto the down line before setting off towards the junction. The wooden signal box, indicative of

unstable ground due to mining, had 54 levers, also controlled the adjacent level crossing and the western end of the loops and sidings.

B. Lord

Above: Bickershaw Junction, 1964. Going in the opposite direction to the picture on page 48 with a load of empties is Black Five No.44958 on 1 July. The line off under the bridge is to Scowcroft, Scowcroft sidings, and Hindley Green station. The set of signals is interesting. The smaller arm is for the route to Moss Hall Colliery and was bi-directional to allow trains from there, after reversal, to pass along the main line. The left-hand arm is to proceed along to Platt Bridge Junction and thence to Wigan North Western. Alternatively, it could pass along the former Lancs. Union line to Ince Moss Junction and so gain access to Bamfurlong sidings or the line to St. Helens. The middle arm will allow the train to pass under the main line to Hindley & Platt Bridge Junction (GCR) and via the Amberswood junctions, to the Whelley loop and the north.

Allan Heyes

51

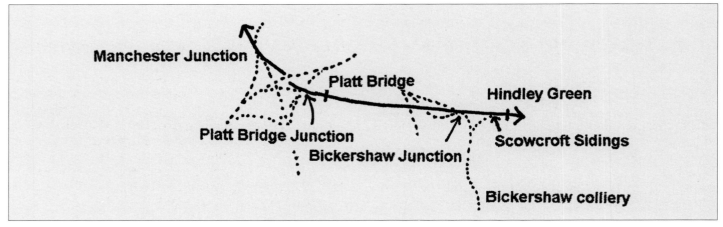

Above: The London & North Western line to Platt Bridge and Hindley Green

Below: The Lancashire Union line from Red Rock, around Wigan, to Bryn (The Whelley loop)

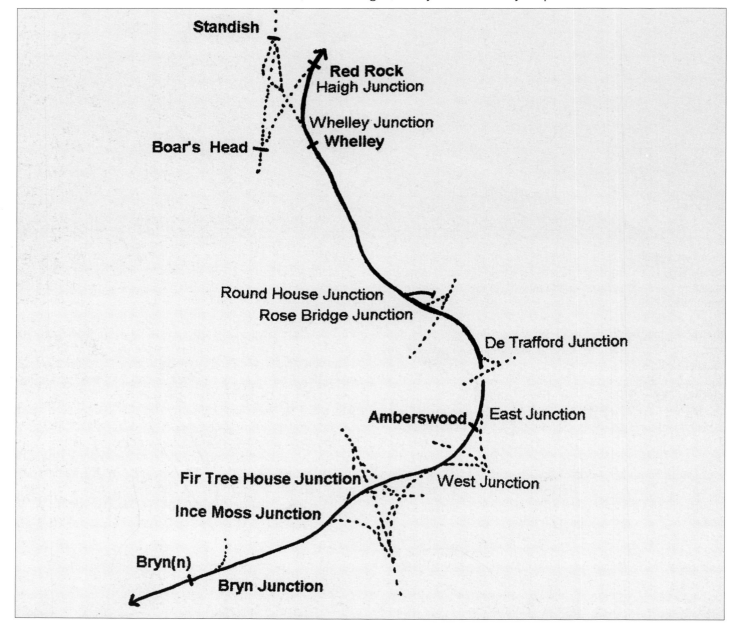

CHAPTER SIX

The Lancashire Union line from Red Rock, around Wigan, to Bryn (The Whelley loop)

Colliery owners around Wigan were dictated to by the L&Y as to the port they could send their coal to – Liverpool. Keen to see competition between railways, as this would enable them to lower their prices, they supported moves to join up with lines to other docks on the Mersey. They also wanted access to towns in north east Lancashire, like Blackburn, Accrington and Burnley as a market for their coal. The 1864 Lancashire Railway Union Act was supported by the L&NWR, for the development of a line from Haigh Junction, north of Wigan on the Boar's Head-Adlington-Blackburn line, around the east of Wigan to curve south, and then west, linking up with that company's lines at St. Helens leading to docks at Widnes/Garston. The LU line reduced the Wigan to Blackburn distance from 27 to 18 miles, to Chorley from 11 to 8 miles and to St. Helens from 13 to 9 miles: as rates were by the mile then the construction costs of £20,000 per mile (£900,000 altogether) were soon recouped.

Above: Whelley Station, remains. A mile from the junction, and south of the Whelley Road overbridge was the site of one of Britain's shortest lived stations. Opening at the start of 1872, it briefly enjoyed a train service to Liverpool – 3 trains per day – until 1 March 1872 when it closed to passengers, although remaining open as a goods station for a great deal longer. This 1969 view north, shows the site of the station and the buildings associated with it. A light engine is passing the station buildings at Whelley nearly one hundred years after it closed to passengers.

John Marshall

Previous page, top: Red Rock station. This opened on 1 December 1869 and jointly owned by the L&Y/L&NWR as part of the short 6 mile link from the North Union Railway at Boar's Head to the L&Y's Bolton to Preston line at Adlington. At the latter station the LU had a line to Cherry Tree, near Blackburn. From 1885 through coaches went from Blackburn to Euston via Chorley and Wigan until 1905 and then they went via Bolton, Manchester Victoria and Stockport. A station was built where Red Rock Lane crosses the Leeds to Liverpool canal. This view is along the Chorley platform, just before the station closed completely in 1957. The station had staggered platforms, and in its heyday, according to a 1911 timetable, only had a sparse service, 8 trains per day each way. What this also shows is that the L&Y had a slightly longer route to Chorley which had slightly more trains. Between them, there was almost a hourly train from Wigan to Blackburn. The Red Rock service stopped soon after the war (September 26th 1949) and the Blackrod route in the late 1960s.

H.C. Casserley

Previous page, bottom: Haigh Junction. The view here is along the line from Red Rock to Boars Head, with the single line going south to Whelley Junction. Originally this was double, but it declined in importance and was singled in 1952, closing in 1967. Connections used to go down to Haigh saw mills.

J Peden collection

Above: Haigh Cutting. South of Whelley station and the line passes through the lands of the Earl of Crawford & Balcarres, close to Haigh Hall. A condition for the building of the line was that it went into a tunnel to avoid it being visible from the stately home. However, the 374 yard tunnel was never more than a few feet from the surface and an ornamental pond was built on top. The land continually subsided and in 1883 it was opened out.

J Peden collection

Above: Kirkless colliery and iron works were developed on the land between the NUR's Springs Branch and the Leeds-Liverpool canal – which it almost paralleled. There were collieries in the area before the joining of the canals at Top Lock in 1816, this method of transport stimulated their production. As the coal made good quality coke, it was decided from 1850 to build an iron works to the south of the colliery. The number of coke ovens rose to 280 in 1865 and to 460 just eight years later. Blast furnaces also increased from 2 in 1859, to 4 the next year, finishing up with 10 in 1873. At that time coal mined locally amounted to about 2.5 million tons with up to 150,000 tons of pig iron produced. From 1880 steel manufacturing started with furnaces and a rolling mill. Land to the east of Springs Branch was used as slag tips and from 1869 connections with the LU at Round House Junction were made so that an elevated rail system allowed coke, iron ore and limestone to arrive at a higher level for the furnaces. Amalgamations by 1865 led to the formation of the Wigan Coal and Iron Co. employing 10,000 people by the late 1880s. To give some idea of the scale of their operations, they had 5,300 wagons together with a fleet of 20 locomotives and 70 boats. After the turn of the century local coal mining went into decline, however, the iron and steel business went on. The Great War provided a badly needed boost to the industry. A plant was set up to deal with the slag which was a valuable resource. The Flag Works made paving slabs while the Bristol Basic Slag Co. made fertilizer from it. Rail connections were via Rose Bridge Junction and an adjacent tarmacadam had connections to both LU and L&NWR lines. After the Great War the industry once again went into steep decline and in 1927 steel making stopped and 2 years later the furnaces were working at half capacity. Amalgamations in 1930 produced the Wigan Coal Corporation Ltd. and the Lancashire Steel Corporation – the latter rationalising the industry with the closure of the Kirkless plant. The rail connections were cut back too, with the tarmacadam plant restricted to the Springs Branch from 1938-58. When this was cut back between Belle Green Lane and Kirkless Hall Junction, the connection with the LU was reinstated from Rose Bridge Junction, until finally closing in 1965.

This aerial view was taken shortly before closure. Only 2 blast furnaces are in operation, as evident by the smoke from their chimneys. Above them are the coking plants. The springs Branch runs behind the tall chimney from left to right, with the canal near the bottom paralleling it. The high level railway supplying the works, the storage sidings and slag tips make up the railway extent of a once busy industrial area. *J Peden collection*

Above: Round House Sidings, 1965. Being given the right of way is Stanier 8F 2-8-0 No.48730 on 17 July. The water tank, off set signal and the track bed are testimony to a rail network having seen better times. *B.G. Barlow/J Peden collection*

Below: De Trafford Junction signal box. Opening at the same time as the line, 1 December 1869, was this small – but very useful – link to the L&Y at Hindley on its Manchester Victoria to Wigan line. Named after a local stately home, there was quite a volume of traffic that passed on its way to Kearsley Power station, near Bolton. The coal trains would depart from Bamfurlong sorting sidings, accessed from the southern part of the LU line. There would be an engine at each end of the train and it would set off, in reverse. When it arrived at de Trafford Junction most of the train, minus what was the engine at the front, set off for Bolton along the link to the L&Y line. *Robert Humm collection*

Right, top: Amberswood East Junction, 1964. For 10 years after opening the LU line simply curved its way gently south-west. In 1879 the Wigan Junction Railway arrived just south of Amberswood goods yard. This was a line from the CLC main line at Glazebrook, attempting to reach Wigan to start with. By the next year connections had been laid down to make north-east and south-east movements possible. Some Manchester Central, and further afield from the GC system, trains for Blackpool used this route. Six years later, further connections were made from the WJR, but this time to the L&NWR's Wigan to Manchester line. These connections allowed trains from Manchester's Exchange station access to the Wigan avoiding line. Struggling up the curve from the ex-GC line is Class Five No.45376 on 2 September, assistance is provided at the rear by 'Austerity' No.90148. In front will be the East Junction and a route around Wigan to join the WCML at Standish. *B.G. Barlow/J. Peden collection*

Right, bottom: Amberswood West Junction, 1964. 'Crab' 2-6-0 No.42846 is just about to pass over the West Junction, while its last wagons are still passing over the bridge with the ex-GC line to Wigan Central. The curve to the right connects the two at Hindley & Platt Bridge Station. At Amberswood West junction not only were there the connections to the WJR but, by a southerly curve of approximately half a mile, the LU line connected to the L&NWR main line at Bamfurlong, opening in 1889. The main sorting sidings here are on the west of the main line and so the line from the LU passes down and under them to allow transfers between the two lines without causing any of the hold-ups that a normal flat junction would. Trains to and from many of the sorting sidings, works and collieries would have been marshalled here. *B.G. Barlow/J. Peden collection*

Above: Fir Tree Junction, 1966. Passing west with a train load of coal wagons is Stanier 8F 2-8-0 No.48708. The main LU line passes over the L&NWR main line, almost at right angles. Virtually on top of the bridge is Fir Tree Junction. This allowed easterly trains on the LU line to descend sharply to join the L&NWR's Wigan to Eccles line. It would have been across this junction that banana trains to Scotland would pass. In 1912, Elder Fyffes transferred the handling of this fruit from Manchester to Garston. There the port put in up to date methods of transferring to trains from 1929 making it the premier port for the product. Three trains would leave west (at 13.30, 16.00 and 18.00) and would pass along the LU to Standish Junction for the north of England and Scotland. Under the banner of 'perishables' they were hauled by mixed traffic or passenger locos.   *Ray Farrell*

Below: Platt Bridge Junction line, 1970. On its way from Amberswood to Platt Bridge, the Junction line passes under the L&NWR's Wigan to Eccles line. This view is looking south with

the main line on top and the LU line underneath, the signal box controlling both lines. In this view, the box is adjacent to the higher level Manchester line. At the lower level are the Whelley loop lines from Amberswood West Junction. Under the bridge, these lines curve west as goods lines to burrow under the main Wigan to Warrington line and on to Bamfurlong sorting sidings. While the up Whelley lines to Bamfurlong Junction can be seen branching off under the bridge, the down line has been removed. The 'D' on the fine lattice signal post indicated that a 'phone was available for the engine driver to talk to the signal man. The CWS opened up a new glass bottle factory to the east of the up Whelley line in 1955. When electrification arrived in the early 1970s the opportunity was taken to rationalise the track layout. To get to the plant in 1988, a train took the old down burrowing line from Bamfurlong towards Platt Bridge. There is then a reversal after passing under the West Coast main line onto the old up junction line followed by another reversal into the premises now owned by the Rockware Glass Co.   *M.A. King*

Right: Ince Moss Junction 1969. This centenary view is east toward Fir Tree House Junction, in the distance, from Ince Moss Junction. Here the LU line met two others. From the right arrive the lines from Bamfurlong sidings and adjacent colliery: from the left is a curve from the L&NWR's main line from Wigan. Originally the gradient down to this junction on the LU line was a stiff 1 in 86. Over time Ince Moss junction sank faster than the surrounding lines resulting in it becoming a steep 1 in 42. Banking engines, often 0-8-2s from Springs Branch shed, were needed if a train consisted of more than 35 wagons. Coal trains for Garston docks, often destined for Ireland, were marshalled at Bamfurlong and then would pass around the curve to Ince Moss on their way via the LU line. They would go via the Black Brook branch and so avoid St. Helens station. At their peak, in the first decade of this century, around 20 trains per day made this trip.   *John Marshall*

Above: Shunting engine, 1952. These tank engines were introduced by C.J. Bowen-Cooke, thirty being built between 1911-17 for heavy shunting. Basically, they were a tank version of the G class 0-8-0 engine with a rear pony truck. The third pair of driving wheels were flangeless and the coupling rod had two joints in it to allow sharp curves to be negotiated. Originally they were fitted with long/narrow buffers (13″ head), but due to locking on sharp curves they were replaced by Webb standard 18″ head buffers. The number, in L&NWR days, was where 'LMS' is on this example. In common with engines from the same pedigree, it carried no smoke box number. There were three rear cab windows and behind the middle one was the water filler. During refuelling, it often became covered by coal and so later was raised up. *N. Stead*

Bryn Junction, 1964. A loaded Long Meg – Widnes anhydrite train slogs up the gradient, with the help of a banking engine at the rear, just over two miles west of Wigan on 31 July. The crossovers allowed interchange between fast (on the left) and slow lines. Onto the latter were connections from adjacent collieries at Bryn Hall Sidings, Garswood Hall Sidings as well as Park Colliery at Garswood.

Allan Heyes

Above: Garswood Hall Colliery, pits 5, 6 & 7. Garswood Hall Collieries took over operations at the many pits in the Bryn area from 1929. One such operation, Park Lane Colliery, illustrates the changing fortunes of the area. This was connected to the Pemberton branch and in the early 1880s was employing 2,000 people. By 1929, after the merger it was closed down. Such rationalisations were partly because the coal was worked out and also because connections with adjacent collieries meant that the number of openings could be reduced. Garswood Hall Colliery remained in production until 1958 and up to 1962 as a washery.

J. Ryan/J Peden collection

Below: Bryn, formerly Brynn. On a straight run from Wigan is the station of Bryn, for Ashton in Makerfield, opening, like the rest of the line on November 1st 1869 (passengers a month later). Just before the station was the junction with the same name leading to the double track Pemberton branch. This passed north to the colliery with the same name, and, beyond the L&Y line to Liverpool, to

Norley Hall Colliery. This was originally connected to the L&Y line from 1860 but tended to use the LU connection from 1871. Before finally closing in l914 the colliery closed first in 1896/7, reopening in 1906/8. Coal trains could get onto the L&Y line from this branch via Goose Green and Pemberton junctions. This view shows the station in 1911, looking towards Wigan. The 1865 Act stated that the L&NWR were to run the line, with the L&Y having access to St. Helens. The L&NWR finally absorbing the line on July 7 1882. This and the next station along the line, Garswood, illustrate the LU 'style' – if there is one: the buildings have some similar features, which is not surprising as they were tendered for and built by the same builder, Fairclough & Sons. Bryn station is adjacent to a main road and steps led down to the platforms. Traffic was so heavy on the section from Ince Moss Junction to Carr Mill, near St. Helens, that two extra lines were added to the south in 1892. The additional lines are behind the Liverpool platform to the right, and they can be seen under the bridge: there was no passenger connection to them.

J Ryan/J Peden collection

Above: Garswood, 1969. Reduction in wagon loads has led to a return to the days before 1892 with dismantling of the goods lines. By the time of this photo. the canopies had been removed. The route that the line took wasn't the one planned by the Lancashire Union Railway in the mid 1860s. Their route was further south crossing the North Union Line at Bamfurlong and then through Haydock and Ashton. A rival line was proposed at that time, put forward by the South Lancashire Railway & Dock Company, to go through Bryn and Garswood on its way via St. Helens, Prescott and Childwall to get to new docks at Dingle: it was the latter route that the LU settled on.

Mowat collection

Below: Park Colliery. 'Hornet' shunts some wagons at Park Colliery, owned by J&R Stone from 1909 until nationalisation in 1947, finally closing in 1960. This was connected to the LU lines from 1870 and after they were widened, to the goods lines adjacent to Garswood Station.

J. Peden collection

CHAPTER SEVEN

The Great Central line to Wigan, via West Leigh, Bickershaw, Hindley and Ince

The Cheshire Lines Committee opened its own line between the two largest cities in Lancashire in 1873, and set about attempting to prise the monopoly of rail traffic from the L&NWR and the L&Y. To help in this process the MS&LR and the MR supported the Wigan Junction Railway. This was to go from Glazebrook, on the CLC main line, to Wigan. With many colliery connections it would tap into Lancashire's coal fields. The line was constructed in three parts. Initially it went north as far as Strangeways and was goods only. Five years later, in 1884, it was extended to the outskirts of Wigan, to Darlington Street, and carried both goods and passengers. It would be another eight years before the line made the final half a mile to central Wigan.

Above: West Leigh and Bedford station. Opening as a passenger station in 1884 it was called Plank Lane for Bedford. However, with the L&NWR opening its West Leigh branch, and subsequently developing Plank Lane station on it, the WJR changed the name of its station. In the 1873 draft plan there was to be a branch to West Leigh. Objections from the L&NWR, as this conflicted with their own plans, meant that this part didn't appear in the final Act. This illustrates well the opportunities for multiple connections to the numerous pits and lines. Eventually, a connection was built between the WJR and the L&NWR lines, as this 1951 north looking view shows. The line to Wigan is straight on and the line to Plank Lane goes off to the right at the end of the platform. The wooden construction of the undulating platforms and buildings show up well. The signal box, Bickershaw Junction, had 24 levers and controlled the 1879 WJR line to Plank Lane. There it met the L&NWR's extension west from Pennington Junction, both seeking access to Bickershaw Colliery. *Stations UK*

Right: Bickershaw and Abram station. A south looking view in the 1950s of the simple passenger platforms dating from 1884. Half a mile north and the line passes under the L&NWR Eccles to Wigan line via Tyldesley, and junctions were made between the two. As the map shows, these were anything but simple. The up line leaves the L&NWR line and proceeds to burrow underneath it. A meeting with the down line occurs, and together they make a simple double junction with the WJR line. Lines to collieries further complicate matters. A 22 lever signal box was behind the photographer, it controlled the level crossing and movements along the line until closure in 1965. *Stations UK*

Above: Hindley and Platt Bridge station. It was to just under the bridge that the line opened in 1879 with connections to Strangeways Hall Colliery. The wooden buildings and booking office, accessed from Stony Lane, opened in 1884. The station started life as Strangeways & Hindley until 1 January 1891. The name became Hindley & Platt Bridge until 1 July 1950 when it became Hindley South. Finances of the WJR were extremely precarious in the early years: 1880 (second half) receipts of £931; 1881 loss of £2,614; 1882 (first half) receipts of £3,029. A far from profitable venture – hence the need to press on to Wigan. Although the Great War was over, the pre-war custom of painting things, e.g. platform edges white for safety in the blackout,

continues. The impressive signal gantry protects the junctions north of the station. South of the station at Strangeways East Junction was the 1886 Hindle Junction line from Bickershaw Junction on the L&NWR's Eccles to Wigan line. *Stations UK*

Left: Hindley and Platt Bridge Junction, 1951. Controlling the lines north, along the ex-WJR to Wigan, and the connections put in during the 1880s to the Lancashire Union line, opened in 1869, (on the embankment in the background) was the function of this over-50 lever wooden signal box. The 1886 connection to the right, Amberswood North curve, was to the LU and to Whelley and the north, to join the L&NWR West Coast main line at Standish Junction. It would have been along this route that trains from Stockport and the rest of the GC system travelled on their way to Blackpool. The 1881/2 connections to the left, Amberswood South Curve, were onto the LU line to St. Helens and to the L&NWR main line south at Bamfurlong. Interestingly, it was the colliery company that built the ground works up to ballast level, with the WJR laying the track. Notice the mirror on a pole so that trains in the station can be seen.

Signalling Record Society, Scrimgeour collection

Right: Hindley South, 1964. Arriving on 1 July is the 2pm ex-Wigan Central all stations to Manchester Central, a journey that would take approximately an hour. The service from Wallgate would take half that time illustrating the different provisions of the services. The five coaches are being hauled by Stanier 2-6-4T No.42631. The first coach is an interesting one. Not only does it have the electrification warning flashes, but also end windows and a small 'lookout' in the guard's compartment. *Allan Heyes*

Above: Lower Ince Station, 1964. 'Black Five' 4-6-0 No.44671 is in charge of the 1pm from Wigan to Manchester Central on 12 July, this journey would take just over 45 minutes. It was built at Horwich in February 1950 at a cost of £14,175, being withdrawn just seventeen years later. Illustrating inflation, this was more than twice the cost of the first of its sister engines back in 1934. In keeping with most railway and bus undertakings now, there were better facilities for passengers' protection on the busiest side. Residents of Junction Terrace had a good view of the line, built in 1884. Through connections from Wigan to places like London were advertised, even though they were hopelessly uncompetitive in time and distance. *Stations UK*

Below: Lower Ince Shed. This shed was opened by the Wigan Junction Railway in 1879 and operated by the MS&LR and its successor, the GCR. As the main reason for the line's existence was freight traffic, it is not surprising that well known passenger loco. types were seldom seen here. Originally built as a dead end two road shed it was modified to be a through shed during the war, as this 1953 view shows. The photographer is looking east showing the water tower just above the shed's lean-to, towards Lower Ince Signal box. To the left is the L&Y's line at Ince from Manchester to Wigan Wallgate. Oddly enough, the shed never had a turntable. The nearest was half a mile north along the line to Wigan, just before the line crossed the canal to the Darlington Street depot. Race meetings at nearby Haydock Park saw engines coming here for servicing and turning in readiness for the return trip. It closed on 22 March 1952, the remaining engines transferring to Springs Branch shed. *IRS/Brian Webb collection*

Right, top: Wigan Central Station, circa 1905. In 1884 the line was extended from Strangeways to Darlington Street, and again in 1892 to Central station. The previous site became a goods shed. This fine old photograph shows the intended layout well. Double track was used until soon after the Great War when the up line became two long sidings. Single line workings were in operation from Wigan Goods Box – at the southern end of Darlington Street depot. There was a small bay on the up side, occupied by some six-wheel coaches and two small adjacent sidings. The railway staff are looking at coaches that have come from the Glazebrook direction along what was intended to be the up through line. On the down side there was a wide island platform with a carriage siding next to it. As this was to be a terminus, if only for the short term, then engine release crossovers were provided. With the opening of the line to Central station the number of third class passengers rose from 70,000 (in the half year of 1884) to 122,000 for the same period in 1897. *John Ryan collection*

Below: Wigan Central, 1964. Compared to the earlier view, much of the railway infrastructure appears to be intact. Even though the island platform went some time ago, the long distinctive canopy and the two water tanks were still in existence.   *B. Hoper collection*

Above: Taking water, 1952. The main way that the branch was operated was by trains to and from Manchester Central, Irlam, Flixton or Glazebrook. At Wigan the engine could run round the coaches and then attach to the front in readiness for the return trip; unless going to be serviced at Lower Ince shed. Here, J10 0-6-0 No.65170 has arrived on 23 August and is refilling the tender before the journey south. The island platform had been removed and a ground frame, operated by the station staff, has meant the removal of the signal box and signals. The journey to Glazebrook, 8 miles, or to Manchester Central, 21 miles, starts off on the same line as it had arrived on as far as the line crossing the canal and Wigan Goods signal box. From there, normal double track arrangements existed. *R.M. Casserley*

Below: Station buildings, street side, 1960. This imposing structure was built to house a railway that didn't materialise. One can imagine the scores of passengers making their way to the entrance in Station Road to board GCR trains to Blackpool. Even the

chimneys are ornate. In reality, only the left-hand part was used for railway business. The part with the distinctive cupola was, in the 1960s, a bathroom showroom. 'Baby' Austin, Ford Popular and a Riley were the small family cars of the day. Unemployment was practically negligible and with plenty of jobs, wages rose. So did people's expectations. Cheap 'package' holidays abroad came along together with motorway building. Without a transport plan then Darwin's 'survival of the fittest' (or market forces as it is now dressed up) came into play and so the line closed on 2 November 1964. *N.D. Mundy*

Right: Final days. When the line opened to Darlington Street with passenger services in 1884, residents of Wigan were probably under the impression that an extension into the town's centre would soon be built. However, they little realised the railway politics of the Victorian age. The ambitions of the MS&LR's Chairman, Edward Watkins, was not to be beaten by the opposition. Hence the CLC line between Lancashire's two great cities. His support for the Wigan Junction Railway was two-fold. Firstly, the southern part of the line was a revenue earner due to the number of collieries, while the northern part had possibilities for development to Preston and Blackpool. The decade from 1882 saw large sums of money spent on fees and land for the line through central Wigan to meet with the West Lancashire Railway at Longton on its Preston-Southport line. A fine bridge over the River Ribble and then on to Blackpool was the plan of the Blackpool Railway Company. Originally, the plans had the Wigan station at Queen Street, but the L&NWR objected saying that the sighting of its signals would be obstructed. and so the Mill Meadow site was compromised on. This is an interesting view from under the canopy. The train has arrived from Manchester Central. Note the wooden platform, the bits either side were brick with flagstones on top, and the absence of the clock.

Eddie Bellass

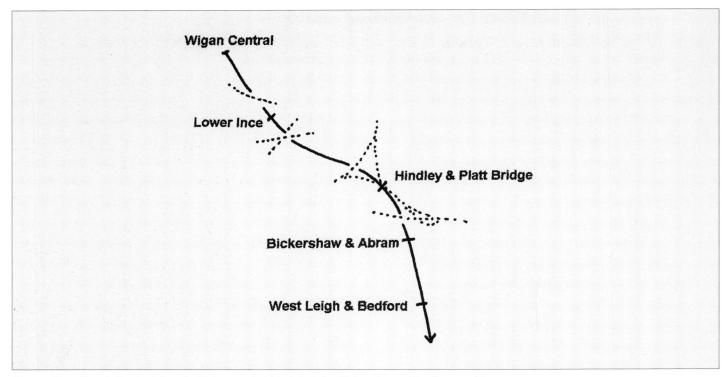

Above: The Great Central line to Wigan, via West Leigh, Bickershaw, Hindley and Ince.

Below: The Lancashire & Yorkshire line via Gathurst, Appley Bridge to Hoscar (The Manchester to Southport line), and the Lancashire & Yorkshire line from Hindley, via Wigan to Rainford Junction (The Liverpool to Bury line).

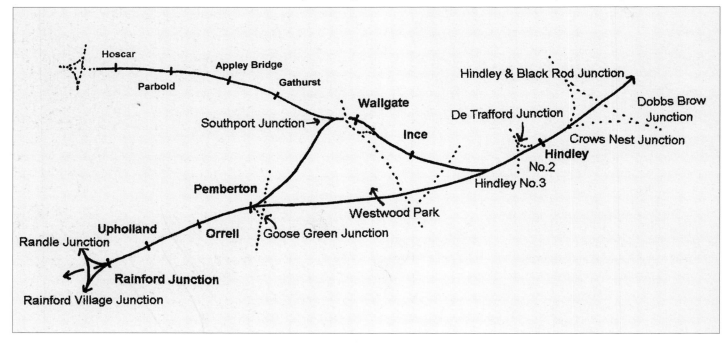

CHAPTER EIGHT

The Lancashire & Yorkshire line via Gathurst, Appley Bridge to Hoscar
(The Manchester to Southport line)

Although opened by the L&Y on 9 April 1855 as far as Burscough Bridge, the line from Wigan to Southport was part of the Manchester & Southport Railway. Their Act of 1847 authorised them to build a line to link the Manchester and Bolton line at Pendlebury with the Liverpool, Ormskirk & Preston Railway at Burscough Junction. Connections to collieries in the Wigan area were also given the go ahead.

In 1848 the Liverpool & Bury line opened via Wigan.

It was from here that the former M&SR line was opened by the L&Y as a single line, to be doubled in 1860/61. Another part of the former M&SR between Burscough Bridge and Southport was jointly developed by the L&Y and the East Lancashire Railway and opened on the same day in 1855. The final part of the ex-M&SR east of Wigan was opened from Hindley to Pendleton in 1888: in effect the line of the M&SR was opened by other railway companies and it never itself ran a train!

Above: Southport Junction. Upon leaving Wigan's Wallgate Station the line passes under the L&NWR's main line. Almost immediately the line splits at Southport Junction: in the fork is Wallgate signal box. The line east, behind the box, is for Southport while the southern fork is for Liverpool. The Liverpool line leaves Wigan on a viaduct, swinging south. On the south side of the Southport line was Prescott Street loco. depot of the L&Y, with its entrance from Cricket Street.
M. Christensen

Right: Wigan Wallgate signal box interior, 1942. Built of material to render it bomb proof is this 1941 modern image box: it is still in use. As well as an internal staircase it had 14" solid brick walls. 12" reinforced flat roof and no locking room windows. When it was commissioned, it took over the duties of Nos. 2 & 3 boxes from the east as well as No 5 box along the Southport line, together with No.4 and Worsley Mesnes boxes on the Liverpool line. In total, the 6 men at the new box replaced 14 men and 2 boys. Although of 'state of the art' design, it looks extremely dark and barren – perhaps bearing in mind the time it is acceptable. The L&NWR stirrup handles were fitted after the box opened. For the number of boxes that were closed when this opened, the number of levers (65) is not great. However, some of the boxes were quite small – No.4 box for example controlled access to a coal yard on the north side.
British Railways

Above: Leaving Wigan, 1965. With the time at about twenty-to-five in the afternoon, the 16.10 from Manchester Victoria to Southport has just restarted from its single stop, at Wigan Wallgate, and is crossing the Leeds-Liverpool canal at Martland Mill ready for a sprint down the shallow gradient. Experiments with Caprotti valve gear were carried out on ten Class Five engines, including this one, No.44757, which is also fitted with a double chimney.   *Allan Heyes*

Below: *Right*: Wigan loco shed. The first shed was opened at Wigan in 1860. A rebuild in 1877 after a fire was too small for the numbers allocated there, similarly after a mid 1880s enlargement to an eight road shed. Subsidence caused its closure in 1905 and the opening of Prescott Street as a fourteen road wooden building, on a brick base, in the northlight style. The track entrance was by means of trailing points from both up and down lines which was later modified. Not long after World War 2 saw the demolition of the front of the southern part of the shed, making it appear like an 'L' shape as this 1961 view shows. Prominent in this view west are 2-6-4T and typical L&Y water columns. An unidentified coach provides some accommodation on the left.   *R.S. Carpenter*

Above: Under the L&Y Wigan was shed code 16 and it wasn't long before over 70 locos. were allocated. Many were 2-4-2T with a large number of 0-8-0s and 0-6-0STs, reflecting the freight and shunting nature of its stock. It also boasted a state of the art 55' electric turntable, which, from 1905, replaced a smaller model. Here is a Fowler modification of the successful G class, No.49515, in May 1954. Many of these 'Baby Austin' engines were outlasted by the L&NWR engines they were designed to replace: poor axlebox bearings were their downfall.
F.W. Shuttleworth

Below: Looking decidedly 'top-heavy' is former L&Y 0-8-0 No.52831 over the inspection bays in the early 1950s. These engines were built under Aspinall's direction and were used as the basis for many experiments by the L&Y's George Hughes. This one has a bigger boiler, giving it an awkward appearance.
L&GRP

Above: Inside shed, 1939. One class well represented in Wigan's loco. stock was the L&Y 0-6-0. In 1939, with its LMS number, is Hughes 3F No.12575. Many loco. sheds had smoke hoods right over the running lines to vent the fumes as quickly as possible: here it drifted to the ceiling before exiting.

R.K. Blencowe

Below: Coaling, 1963. A much welcome, and speedier way for coal to be shovelled from the floor, was onto one of these conveyor belts. In view are a brace of Stanier 2-6-4 tanks, Nos.42631 & 42569. The shed code changed to 23D (1935), to 27D (1953), ending as 8P (1963) until closure a year later.

A.K. Jones collection

Above: Engineering works, south of the line. Various works occupied the area between the railway and the canal from the latter part of the nineteenth century. To the west was the Pagefield Works of Walker Bros., with Wigan Rolling Mills to the east. While they relied upon the connections from Meadow Colliery to begin with, they later developed their own sidings. Steel products were the main items made, with businesses having chequered openings and closings. The two firms co-operated over the internal movements in their works. Here we can see an 0-4-0ST named HARRY (1876-1946) at work hauling wagons from the erecting/machine shops towards the foundry. Controlling movements onto the main line was the signal box at Barley Brook (Wallgate No.5) with 24 levers. *J. Peden collection*

Right: Douglas Bank Signal Box, 1984. From the early 1860s until 1920 coal was mined to the north of the line at Douglas Bank, next to the site of the original engine shed. Controlling movements between the colliery and the main line was this signal box at Douglas Bank. As traffic increased, the 1846, 14 levers, box was replaced by this larger one of 40 levers in 1904. The 1941 resignalling scheme that brought the ARP boxes into being did away with Barley Brook box, with Douglas Bank closing soon after this picture: part of it now resides in Wigan Pier Museum. *G. Earl*

West of Wigan, 1954. For the next few miles west, the line, canal and River Douglas, all make their way through gaps in the rock outcrop revealing some beautiful scenery. Excursions to the seaside were, and still are, big business. While today's trippers get caught in traffic jams, yesterday's trippers caught special trains. The demand was so great that almost anything serviceable was pressed into use. So, at Easter, Stanier 8F 2-8-0 No.48202 is in charge. In spite of small wheels, important in freight locos, it could still put up a fair turn of speed when needed. To enable these engines to work such trains they needed to have the correct balances on the wheels: many wartime built engines were unsuitable. A star under the number on the cabside showed those with adequate reciprocating balance to stop uncomfortable longitudinal shuttling movements. Reporting numbers were not only on engines. but also on the coaches they were to pull – to make sure they set off with the correct ones!

A.G. Ellis

Above: Gathurst. One of the original stations on the line. The first four are very similar with sandstone buildings on the up, to Wigan, platform and wooden shelters on the Southport platform. This 1976 view towards Southport shows no visible means of transferring from one of the staggered platforms to the other. The nature of the terrain necessitates an overbridge at one end of the station while there is an underbridge for the Southport end platform entrance. The shelter is the replacement for a larger wooden one. In 1888 the Roburite Explosives Co. Ltd. opened a factory on the north side of the River Douglas, some way from the station. A narrow gauge railway was laid for internal movement and to a transhipment shed in the station yard. The firm became part of ICI via Nobel's Explosives and it was not until the late 1980s that the sidings were deleted from the traffic lists with the firm preferring to use the roads. The station buildings, having had their layer of grime removed, now function as a public house. *RCTS*

Right: Gathurst signal box, 1965. This was a Saxby and Farmer 15 lever box, lasting not far short of its centenary, closing in 1971. The adjacent overbridge causes sighting problems which were resolved by making the box able to see over the bridge. Prior to the days of power signal boxes, signal cabin staff had to enter train movements into a register and they also checked for tail lamps to make sure trains hadn't split in two. The box had to be at this end of the station due to the arrangement of the goods yard. *L&YR Society*

Above: Appley Bridge station. 1964. Where the road crossed the canal was a convenient place in the undulating terrain to build a station. Many local industries were set up, e.g. quarrying, brickmaking (ceased in 1954) and the mill which made linoleum until the late 1960s, each having their rail connections. From 1981, special container trains brought rubbish from places in Greater Manchester to fill the quarry. This view towards Wigan shows the curved platforms and the typical station buildings, complete with over 100 years of grime. This is now the 'Old Station House' restaurant having been cleaned up and enlarged. To the rear of the buildings is the goods yard, complete with crane. Two new bus stop type shelters provide passenger protection, the original shelter can just be made out behind the brick building. The lamp at the end of the platform was typical of the stations on the line having the name painted along the glass at the top on the front panel. West of the station were some industrial sidings on the south of the line, as well as the up and down loops. Controlling affairs was the West box, a product of the 1876 resignalling of the line. There were originally 29 levers in a Saxby and Farmer frame, but in 1920, 9 were removed: it closed in 1968. A smaller, 15 levers, box controlled events at the east of the station until 1965. *A.G. Ellis*

Left: Appley Bridge, 1964. Hauling a Wigan-Southport non-corridor stock train is Stanier 2-6-0 No.42959. Apart from the Manchester to Southport trains, Wallgate station had a bay especially for this, and locals along the Liverpool line. This loco. was one of a small class (40 locos) that were really Stanier modifications of the highly successful Hughes 'Crabs' and although built at Crewe in 5 months in 1933/34 they are of Horwich origin. The pipe along the boiler was the exhaust pipe from the vacuum ejector which was just in front of the cab. Other LMS Mogul engines were the Ivatts, either with their high running board, 43000 series, or the lightweight version, 46400 series, both of which had smaller driving wheels than the 5'6" of the Hughes and Stanier types. *A.G. Ellis*

Right: Parbold Station, 1972. This is an excellent example of an L&Y country station. The buildings are grouped around the passenger access and there are canopies for protection on both platforms. This view is towards Wigan. *A.J. Sommerfield*

Above: Parbold for Newburgh. This crossing coincides with Parbold station and, as can be seen, there was a subway for people to cross the line when the gates were closed. The cabin was typical of the late 1870s L&Y resignalling scheme. Being given the right of way is Standard class 4 4-6-0 No.75046 heading for Southport in 1965. The engine was built at Swindon in 1953. One innovation developed for Standard class tender engines was to address one problem that firemen had. They had to keep their balance on the cab floor and the front of the tender, with both moving independently of each other! The cab floor was extended backwards so as to come beneath the shovelling plate. One problem the design produced was to make the cab very draughty. Many were fitted with flexible screens between the tender and engine to overcome this.

L&YR Society

Above: Hoscar station, looking east. Although having staggered platforms around a level crossing, the distinctive style of the station buildings makes this out to be one of the original set, it opened as Hoscar Moss. A ticket office and shelter are on the up, Wigan, platform. There are three level crossings in the little over a mile between Parbold and here. Most of the crossing cabins were small wooden affairs with their levers interlocked with the main station boxes. While there was simply a wooden hut on the Southport bound platform, as the booking office was adjacent to the level crossing, passengers would wait there until they got the signal of an approaching Southport train. In the one and a half miles between here and Burscough Bridge, there were level crossings at Shaw and Four Lane Ends, each with their own small cabin. *L&YR Society*

Below: Hoscar water troughs, 1964. West of Hoscar station, the L&Y introduced a set of water troughs. Essentially, what was needed was a practically flat and, ideally, straight piece of track, both conditions being met here. All L&Y tank locos. were fitted with a special pick up gear to enable them to collect water, whichever way they were going. The scoop was vacuum operated. Heading west on 5 August is Stanier 2 cylinder 2-6-4T No.42589. The perception of water troughs is that they enable non-stop running of express trains. On the L&Y their use was somewhat different. Their location generally was on the approach to terminal stations so that engines could arrive with their tanks full, and so reduce the time for servicing. Quite a degree of skill was necessary in winding up the scoop at the appropriate time: too late and the first coach got a good wash (bad luck on any compartments with the window open on a summer's day). Fun as such a practice was, it tended to unsettle the ballast, so causing extra maintenance. *B.G. Barlow*

CHAPTER NINE

The Lancashire & Yorkshire line from Hindley, via Wigan to Rainford Junction
(The Liverpool to Bury line)

In the late 1830s the railway route between Liverpool and Manchester was dominated by the company with that name. An attempt to break that monopoly was made by the Liverpool & Bury Railway. Their line was to make a junction at Walton (with the East Lancs. Railway from Liverpool to Preston). It would then serve the rich Wigan coalfield and make a junction at Lostock (with the North Union Railway line to Bolton), and then to Bury. Other links eastwards would give the company independent access to Yorkshire. It would also offer shorter journeys, from the Wigan area, to both Liverpool, with its docks, and Manchester, than the present set up with the L&M railway via Parkside. The line opened on 20 November 1848 after the company had firstly been absorbed by the Manchester & Leeds Railway (1.10.1846), and subsequently by the Lancashire & Yorkshire Railway (23.7.1847). To the west of Wigan a junction was made with the Burscough Bridge and Southport line when it opened on 9 April 1855. Expansion of the railway network at Hindley to the east, by the L&Y, brought a line from Blackrod (on the NUR line from Lostock to Chorley) to Hindley on 15 July 1868 and later, on 1 October 1888, from Atherton and Manchester. In an attempt to avoid the congestion at Wigan's stations, and to meet the requirement of the coal mines, an avoiding line to the south was opened in 1889.

Dobbs Brow Junction, 1962. Looking east on 16 June sees a Manchester to Blackpool express being hauled by 'Jubilee' class 4-6-0 No.45584 *North West Frontier*. The signals, and the facing point the engine is about to go over, will send the train north to Blackrod. Building of the Westhoughton connecting line between the Atherton and Hilton House lines in 1889 meant that trains for the West Coast from Manchester could avoid both Bolton and Wigan and have their first stop at Preston. Most stopping trains to Blackpool went via Bolton: this was an avoiding line, although note the fairly low speed by today's standard. *Author's collection*

Above: Hindley Station. Opening on 20 November 1848 as a two platform station, it was enlarged by the L&Y to four platforms by the arrival of the Atherton line 40 years later. This is the main entrance from Ladies Lane bridge, straight from the street. A booking office is ahead and then a covered footbridge leads, via steps, down to the platforms. All four lines had some passenger facilities and protection from the elements. However, the roof on the island platform went many years ago. The former fast lines stand derelict, not used and the space practically unusable. The slow platforms are the only two now in use and even the roof has gone. On 1 July 1950 the passenger station became 'Hindley North', reverting some 30 years later back to 'Hindley'. Hindley Green, on the L&NWR line from Wigan to Manchester closed and the GCR station at 'Hindley and Platt Bridge' had changed to 'Hindley South' in 1952 before finally closing in 1964. Hindley was one of only three stations (the other two being Atherton and Pendleton Broad Street) on the line to have platforms on all four running lines. The other stations had only two platforms serving the slow lines which illustrates the nature of the service the L&Y wanted to provide.   *L&YR Society*

Left: Crows Nest Junction, 1956. Just over half a mile east of Hindley station was the site chosen in 1868 from the Liverpool-Bury line for the L&Y's Hilton House branch, the line off to the extreme left. It would meet the NUR line from Bolton to Chorley at Horwich Fork Junction. By this branch, the L&Y, and its allies, would have a route to Preston and Blackburn, independent of the L&NWR. Twenty years later and the L&Y built its direct line to Wigan from Manchester, the lines to the right. This consisted of four lines from Pendleton to Hindley and enlargement of the Hindley area's lines to accommodate such volumes of traffic. For example, the small, 24 lever, 1876 signal box at these junctions – Crows Nest – was replaced by a very large, 92 lever, L&Y box in 1887. The signal box was sandwiched between eight running lines. The Blackrod and Bolton lines were one side, with the four lines to Atherton on the other side. The removal of the Hilton House branch (to Blackrod) and the reduction of the Atherton lines to two means that a simple double junction, complete with new (1.10.1972) signal box now suffices.

Signalling Record Society; Scrimgeour collection

Above: West of Hindley, 1961. Looking east from the fine wrought iron footbridge to the east of the station, adjacent to No.3 box on 16 September, sees 'Austerity' 8F 2-8-0 No.90599 trundling along the down fast with a loaded coal train. It isn't clear whether the route that it will take will be north along the Whelley loop at Box No.2, or west at No.3 box and the Pemberton loop. Either way the separation of goods from congested fast passenger lines will have been achieved. Peering out from underneath the bridge can just be seen the platforms of Hindley North station. The different arches of the bridge show the original lines, to the left, and the later fast lines. No.1 signal box, which was resighted from between the fast and the slow lines in 1956, is partially hidden by the water tank. At that point the up and down directions both had loops as far as No.3 box, just over 500 yards to the west. Waiting at the stop signals, before proceeding onto the up slow line, was a convenient place for engines to take on water. To illustrate the number of pits in the area, one company, Wigan Coal & Iron Co. before 1930, use to run a special test train on a tour of all its weigh bridges to ensure accuracy. Starting at 6am from Hindley it would pass onto the LU line at De Trafford junction and go as far as Standish. *P. Hutchinson*

Below: Hindley No.2, 1964. Arriving at No.2 box from Liverpool is 'Austerity' 2-8-0 No.90233 on 27 August. Just under the gantry, curving away to the right, is the link to De Trafford Junction. It may seem odd that this train is signalled on the up fast line. A short distance west, and the same box could have switched it onto the slow lines, blocking the down fast and the up slow lines in the process. As its route is towards Manchester, at Crows Nest Junction, about a mile to the east, it would have to cross all four tracks. So by delaying the transfer to the up slow until on the Atherton line, the number of conflicting movements is reduced.

B.G. Barlow

Hindley No.2 box, 1965. The impressive signal gantry here was controlled by this 80 lever frame box opened in 1887 ready for the Atherton 'Direct line'. Also at this point, the line north to meet the Lancashire Union Railway, the Whelley Loop, at De Trafford junction branched off. There were extensive sidings, in both up and down directions. It closed in 1972 as the volume in traffic declined. An unidentified Stanier 8F 2-8-0 comes off the Pemberton loop at No.2 box, to the west and is on the up fast line. The wagons are empties from Liverpool's Fazackerley sidings and are on their way to Crofton, near Wakefield in Yorkshire.

Allan Heyes

Above: Ince signal box. This 24 lever in a L&Y tappet frame box was opposite the station offices, on the down side. It survived until 1 October 1972. This was thirty years longer than Ince Hall box just to the west, situated almost on top of the GCR line to Wigan Central. This small 18 lever box existed to control a series of loops on the up side, and a trailing crossover. There were connections to the main line from Ince Hall Coal & Canal's Lower Coal Works, and subsequent operators on the site. In the early 1870s they had 76 coke ovens in operation: Ince was one of the most prolific areas for coal production in the second half of the nineteenth century. This firm was one of those in the early days that were able to work their own train and locos. over the main line railways. Coal trains went to Liverpool and in 1852 an employee was killed uncoupling an engine on Sutton Bank near St. Helens Junction. *L&YR Society*

Right: Ince Station. A little over a mile from Hindley the line goes under Green Lane. The island platform station there replaced an earlier station in 1894. The station offices were of brick construction with a fine station clock over the timetable notice board. This view is looking towards Hindley and shows the wide covered access from the road bridge. Under the bridge can be seen a bracket signal. The smaller arm is the distant for Hindley No.3 and indicates the route onto the slow line. The taller post contains the distant for the route onto the fast lines and consists of a distant (for Hindley No.3) and an upper stop arm (Ince's home). Oddly enough, the down line had 4-aspect colour lights.

British Railways

Above: Approaching Wigan, 1961. Going west, the line rises continuously to enable it to pass over the Leeds and Liverpool canal. This puts the L&Y adjacent to, and at the same level as, the L&NWR lines, and so exchanges are possible between them. Passengers can leave either Wallgate or North Western stations and arrive at the same Manchester station by this means. Two days before Christmas witnesses a train arriving along the L&Y lines and about to pass down to Wallgate station. In charge is Hughes-Fowler 'Crab' 2-6-0 No.42925. A gradient post sign can be seen next to the chimney. The train has just passed behind Wigan No. 1 box. This was of Air Raid Precaution design and dates from the 1941 resignalling scheme replacing several large boxes in the area. It controlled mostly the ex-L&NWR lines, and the L&Y from Ince to almost Wallgate station. It too was replaced in 1972 by the power signal box at Warrington, some seven miles south.

A.K. Jones collection

Right: Leaving Wallgate station, 1960. 28 May sees Stanier 2-6-4T No.42444 climbing up the gradient emerging from the bridge under the road and shops on Wallgate with a Manchester bound train of non-corridor stock. Sidings in the goods yard are on the left and the approach to the goods sheds is on the right. In those days it would have taken about 50 minutes for the 18 mile, 11 station, journey to Manchester Victoria. An alternative route, 2 miles longer with 10 station stops, via Bolton took about the same time. The fastest, non-stop, trains did it in 28 minutes. Today, fast trains from Southport take 39 minutes to go to Piccadilly, and onto the airport. Slow trains from the seaside town pass along the Atherton line in approximately a similar time to Victoria, and then Oldham. Five trains per hour travel between the town and the city.

Ray Farrell

Left: Approaching Wigan. Twenty years earlier and this was the view from Wigan No.2 box, looking north. In front is the whole of North Western station. To the right are sidings and, hidden by the signal box, goods sheds. The main L&Y running lines pass under their box No.1, a 54 lever box dating from 1894, swept away in 1941, when North Western station was rebuilt.

British Railways

Left, top: Approaching Wigan, 1950. Coming up the gradient from the Wallgate direction, is LMS 0-8-0 No.49592, a Fowler modification of the successful G class. Many of these engines were outlasted by the L&NWR engines they were designed to replace: poor axle box bearings were their downfall. *J.A. Peden*

Left, bottom: L&Y goods yard, 1954. One of the celebrated Aspinall Class 27 0-6-0 locos. dating from the early 1890s. The signal gantry, with colour lights, is over the lines descending to Wallgate station. The engine is shunting wagons in the coal yard and adjacent goods sheds. Running from left to right is the footbridge from North Western station to King Street. This area is now the car park. *B. Hoper collection*

Above: L&Y goods yard, 1951. Shunting the coal yard and goods sheds was Barton Wright 0-6-0ST No.51474 in March. The main lines were on a falling westerly gradient under Wallgate to the passenger station of that name to its west. The goods facilities were in two parts, either side of the main running lines. Between them, and the adjacent L&NWR station, were sidings and a coal yard with the footbridge from King Street going across the top of them. This is now a car park, with the part of the bridge across the running lines still in use. Also accessed from Wallgate, but to the north, was the entrance to the two goods sheds the L&Y owned. The engine started life as an 0-6-0 goods tender engine class 23 introduced by Barton Wright from 1877. With Aspinall's more powerful 0-6-0 locos becoming more plentiful from 1890 the decision was made not to scrap these engines, but to convert them. The method was to fit a saddle tank over the boiler, lengthen the rear main frame a little to accommodate the bunker, and fit a cab over the footplate. This proved to be a good idea based upon a well planned engine, with the last one surviving until 1964, many lasting well over 50 years as conversions. Their size and power made them useful engines for the sorting sidings in the south Lancashire area. *B. Hoper collection*

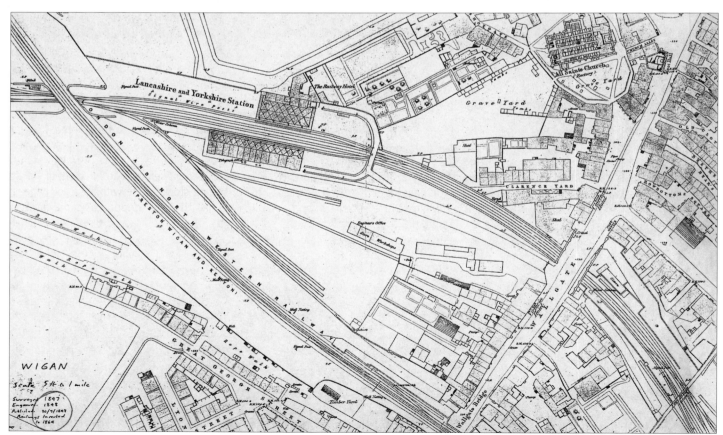

Left, top: Wallgate Station entrance, 1908. The original 1848 station was east of the L&NWR overbridge with its access to the north from Droning Street, and to the south along a long lane from Wallgate. It consisted of two platforms, joined by a wide curved passageway. To compete with the new L&NWR station opened in 1894, the L&Y enlarged and rebuilt their station a short distance to the east, closer to the town centre. The buildings are instantly recognisable today, although cars and street paraphernalia now dominate the scene. While architecturally unlikely to win an award, the style is indicative of a way of life: foot way access and a fair sized covered area for passenger protection. Upon entering the building there is a booking office and then a wide set of steps down to the single island platform. Up to 1924 it was known as the L&Y station, only when both stations were under the control of the LMS was the 'Wallgate' added.   *J. Ryan collection*

Left, bottom: Layout of the original Wallgate Station.

Above: Wallgate station, 1960. In the original plans, a line was to leave Ince, join the NUR and to use their station. Afterwards it was to pass along the north bank of the canal and to Appley and Burscough, ending at Southport. It didn't turn out quite like that! After leaving Ince, the line skirts the L&NWR, dips down, and at the western end of the station, the running lines are squashed together as they go under the WCML. This view is looking east and shows the station layout well. A single island platform, and avoiding loops in both directions, together with a bay at the Southport end, coped with the passenger side of business. To the south were sidings for storing stock – here with some carriages in them, and a loading bay. As the loco. depot was some distance away to the west, a small, 50 foot, turntable was put in. The collection of small wooden huts on the left marks the site of the original station with the stone passageway leading up from them: this use to be the method of crossing the line between the two platforms. There is a hive of activity going on. Arriving under the bridge is a class 5 with a train from Southport while a stopping train waits in the bay. Often trains to Southport and Liverpool Exchange, from Bolton and Manchester, met here to enable passengers to make connections. Simmering in the sidings is the station pilot. The use of a continuous pilot meant that the engine was away from its home shed for longer than a day with loco. crews signing on and off here. It cost £94 to build the services for the pilot engine in June 1911. Also visible is the small turntable.

Ray Farrell

Left, top: Wallgate services, 1955. One journey that is only possible today with a trip to Manchester Victoria, is from the stations between Liverpool via Wigan, Bolton and Bury to Rochdale, and access to Yorkshire. Here we see the 11am departure on 26 August behind BR Standard class 4 4-6-0 No. 75019. It would travel the 19 miles to Liverpool Exchange in 25 minutes. The roadway on the right was part of the access to the down platform of the original station. The extensive roof is not providing much protection and soon would be cut back to around the platform buildings. *Brian Morrison*

Left, bottom: Wallgate services, 1948. Waiting to depart with the 4.9 stopping train to Liverpool is ex-L&Y 0-6-0 No.12598 from shed 23D (Wigan). To call at the 10 stations would take 50 minutes. Today, the hourly trains, with an obligatory change at Kirkby takes the same time to Central station. The 1948 service included a five minute wait at Rainford Junction to enable passengers from St. Helens (dep 4.12) as well as Ormskirk (dep 4.10) and Skelmersdale (dep 4.20) to make connections. *W.A. Camwell*

Right: Wigan No 3 box. Just under the bridge and the lines split to Southport and Liverpool. Controlling events was this odd signal box, dating from the early 1870s. The bay window was added in 1879 when a smaller box, known as 'Churchyard Intermediate'

closed. It was renamed No.3 in 1894 and replaced in 1941. The view through the bridge provides us with a glimpse of Wigan's first L&Y station. The up platform can be seen, also the 'Railway Hotel' and part of the station buildings. *Unknown*

Above: Wallgate's west end, looking east, 1960. Sorting empty stock on 28 May is one of the Hughes-Fowler 'Crab' 2-6-0s. Above the covered van is the remains of the track way that connected the platforms of the original station. *Ray Farrell*

Above: Wigan avoiding lines. Class Five 4-6-0 No.45412 is coming off the Wigan avoiding line at Pemberton Junction with a Bolton to Liverpool football special on 23 April 1966. Opened on 1 May 1889 for goods (passengers a month later), the Pemberton loops passed from Hindley in the east to Pemberton in the west. The 'switch back' allowed express trains to save something like 10 minutes by avoiding Wallgate station and so the L&Y could compete for the Lancashire-Yorkshire traffic even though the route was longer and more steeply graded. Dirt from the nearby Crow Orchard Colliery was used for constructing part of the embankments. In 1911 there was intense competition for the Liverpool-Manchester traffic. Three of the biggest railway companies all took the same time, 40 minutes. However the distances weren't all the same. The L&NWR was the shortest at 31 miles, followed by the GCR at 34 miles. Not surprisingly, the L&Y was proud of its almost hourly Liverpool, Leeds and Bradford and other towns east of the Pennines, trains, covering the 37 miles between the towns in the same time as its rivals, both ways. To give some idea of the toll the war took of the railway system can be seen by looking at their 1951 timings. All three pre-grouping companies, now part of BR, took longer, with only the former L&Y providing a regular non-stop service, but now it took 47 minutes. The ex-L&NWR line usually included a stop at Earlestown or Newton, lengthening the time to between 42 and 50 minutes.

Most former GCR trains stopped at Warrington and needed between 47-52 minutes. Several collieries connected with the line, with loops and sidings being put down at Westwood Park, approximately half way along the loop, lasting until after the war. The avoiding line closed on 14 July 1969. These signal posts, curiously of different designs, are tall to aid sighting. *Allan Heyes*

94

Above: Pemberton Junction, 1963. Arriving at the junction along the original line is LNER Class B1 4-6-0 No.61319 on 8 September on its way from Manchester Victoria to Liverpool Exchange.

I.G. Holt

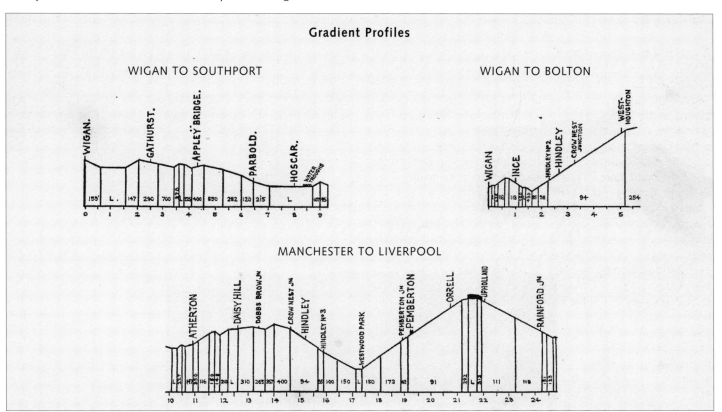

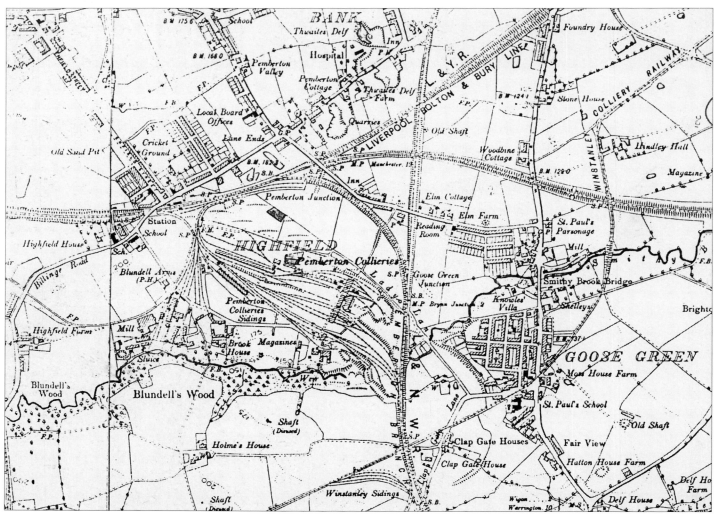

Left, above: Pemberton Junction, looking west, 1966. The development of Wigan's avoiding lines led to the construction of a signal box to control events. The position of the box is not obvious. One would have expected it to be built on the other side of the line where it would have had a better view of all the lines. However, once upon a time, there were four lines joining here. To the west were lines to Pemberton colliery, while to the east there was a connection to the Pemberton branch of the L&NWR. This was a double track line from Bryn (on the LU line) to Pemberton colliery, with the connection to Norley Hall colliery being at Goose Green junction. Although originally connected to the Southport line in 1860, the LU extended its line from the Pemberton branch in 1871. The colliery closed around 25 years later, reopening in 1906, before finally closing in 1914. With the closure of the two mines and the removal of their connecting lines, the signal box looks out of place. This box, 65 levers in an LMS type 11 design, replaced a smaller, 48 levers, Railway Signalling Co. design box in the early 1930s; this too closed, in 1969. To give some idea of the magnitude of mining here, before the Great War, the annual production was in the order of 600,000 tons, the mining company owned 2,000 wagons and there was 15 miles of sidings. The geological faults inherent in the Wigan coalfield meant that it had a short life – being worked out by the 1930s, closing in 1946.
L&YR Society

Left, below: Extract from 6" map of 1889.

Right: Pemberton station, 1966 looking east. Overgrown sidings, evidence of a greater past, are behind the down platform and a one road siding served a goods shed on the up side. In fact coal

was brought here by road to a screening plant from other collieries until the mid 1960s. The cooling tower belongs to Westwood power station.
L&YR Society

Above: Pemberton station, 1966, looking west. This small station opened with the line in 1848. Access is from the adjacent road to the upper storey of the station buildings. Steps lead out onto a footbridge with steps leading down to the platforms. A small wooden shelter is for Liverpool bound passengers, while the Wigan platform has more facilities in a brick building – complete with station clock. The position of the signal post, between the foot and nearby road bridges, means that it has to be tall enough to be seen by drivers.
L&YR Society

Above: Winstanley Colliery sidings. Most railway observers associate this style of loco. with the L&NWR. However the L&Y built almost 150 of these 0-8-0 engines to the design of Aspinall in the second decade of this century. Only a few made it to BR days and only a handful were renumbered by having a 5 replace the 1 at the start of the number. This must be one of the last survivors, shunting in 1951.   *Photomatic*

Below: Winstanley Colliery sidings. Approximately three quarters of a mile west of Pemberton there was a connection to Winstanley Colliery, sorting sidings as well as up and down loops. Signal boxes controlling things between 1875 and 1967 were of the same name, in the east, a 25 lever box replaced by the LMS with their type 1, and, at the Liverpool end, a 30 lever box in a Saxby and Farmer frame. Waiting to leave the sidings to go towards Wigan

is Fowler 0-8-0 No.49563 alongside the conveniently placed water tank. Having the right of way, pulling an equally empty train of wagons is sister engine, No.49582, in April 1951. The L&Y's 1899 Act was for the widening of its lines from Walton Junction to Pemberton Junction. It was to be done in stages as loops at Ditton Brook/Holland Moss, Rainford Colliery/Simonswood and Orrell/ Winstanley. The expensive tunnelling at Upholland and bridge/ viaduct/embankments were problems to be addressed 'later' – the intervention of the Great War meant that this was 'never'.

R.K. Blencowe

Right, top: Orrell East, 1952. Passing along the down main is one of the successful 4F 0-6-0 No.44418 hauling a mixed train, mostly of coal wagons. The gradient from Wigan on the five mile stretch up to Upholland Tunnel is never less than 1 in 90, hence the need for catch points in the Wigan direction to stop runaway wagons. The signals protecting the merger of the main and loop lines stand out proudly with the parachute water tank for the loop line. The lower quadrant loop signals were replaced by LMS style ones by 1954. The yellow fronted, with a black chevron, lower signal on each post is the distant for the box in front, namely Orrell West. The top, red stop, signals are operated by the adjacent box, Orrell East. So a train with a clear road from both boxes will have, independently, both signals pulled 'off'. Interlocking of the system will prevent the distant signal being pulled 'off' if the stop signal is 'on', but there is nothing to prevent the reverse i.e. the stop to be 'off' and the distant to be 'on'. This merely tells the driver that his immediate route is clear and that he should be prepared to stop at the next red signal.   *R.S. Carpenter*

Right, bottom: Signal box diagrams by courtesy of the Signalling Record Society.

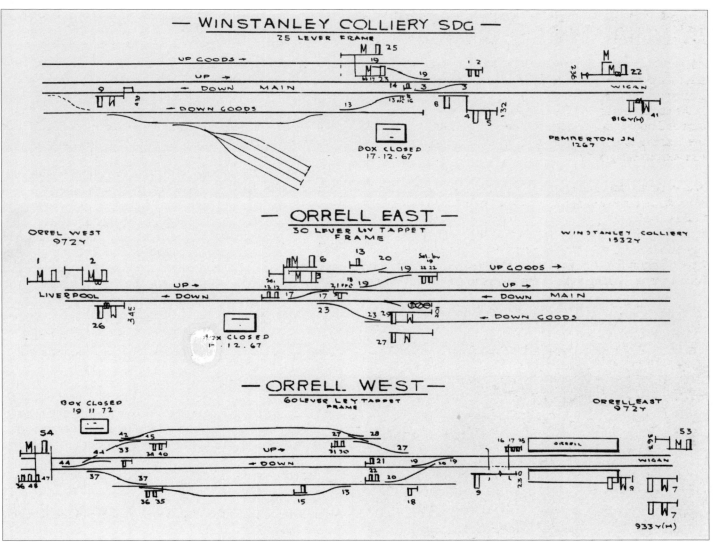

Above: Orrell Station circa 1910. This was one of the original stations on the Liverpool & Bury Railway line, almost 4 miles from Wigan. It was renamed 'Orrell and Upholland' on 1 September 1882, only to revert to the shorter name on 13 October 1900. Even though there was an adjacent road bridge, a covered footbridge was provided. This leads from a booking office of typical L&Y two coloured design. The Wigan bound passengers had the benefit of a substantial wooden shelter, complete with fire places. There were fewer passengers expected in the Liverpool direction hence the bus stop type shelter. Under the bridge the up and down goods loops can just be made out.   *Stations UK*

Left: Orrell West signal box, 1971. To the west of the station were short up/down loops and goods yards. The 60 lever frame box had a year's life left.   *M.A. King*

Right, top: Upholland tunnel. The only way to overcome the solid outcrop of rock was to build this 950 yard tunnel. At the eastern end were these lovely L&Y lower quadrant signals.   *D. Ibbotson*

Right, bottom: Upholland tunnel, 1950. With smoke still lingering at the tunnel mouth, LMS 'Crab' 2-6-0 No.42844 heads east in November. In spite of nationalisation some years earlier and the engine having its BR number, its ill-fitting tender still has its former owners name on it.   *RAS Marketing*

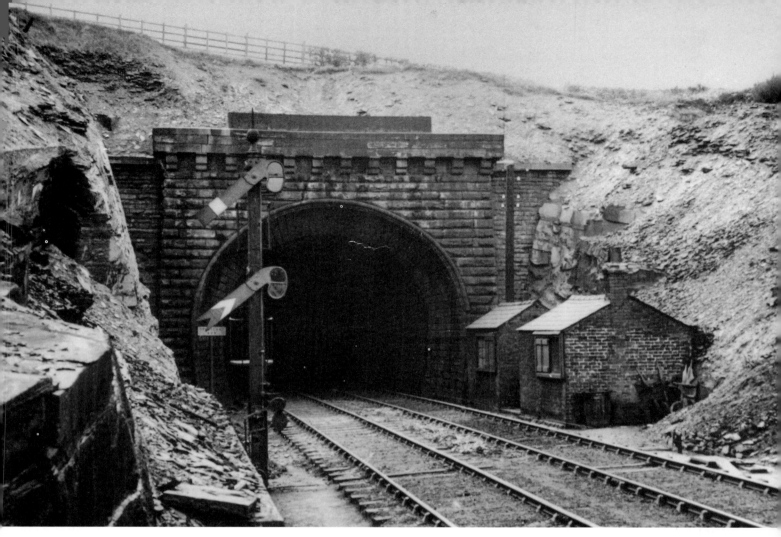

Above: A station opened to the east of the tunnel, about 600 yards west of Orrell station, under the name of Upholland. Another station, Pimbo Lane opened about 400 yards west of the tunnel. Upholland station failed to appear in the 1852 timetable and its name was transferred to the renamed Pimbo Lane station in 1900. This view is east towards the tunnel. Steps lead down to the platforms from the adjacent overbridge. After the closure of the line from Ormskirk to Rainford Junction, and in keeping with the New Town image, the station name boards here read 'Alight here for Skelmersdale', in the 1970s.   *L&Y Railway Society*

Right: Ditton Brook Sidings. Midway between Upholland and Rainford Junction are the colliery connections from Holland Colliery. The goods loops and sorting sidings were controlled by the 44 levers in a L&Y frame at Ditton Brook box in the east.   *C.H.A. Townley*

Right, below: Holland Moss Box, 1956. Three quarters of a mile away, controlling the western end of the loops and the connections to collieries was this small (24 levers) box. The upper arm of the signal is off (Holland Moss's home). The lower arm is also off (Ditton Brook's distant), indicating that the next home signal is also off.

C.H.A. Townley

Left: Upholland tunnel, 1964. Having just struggled up the last seven miles of ever stiffening gradient, the last two miles from Rainford Junction being at least 1 in 118, the footplate crew can now look forward to four miles on a down gradient. This in itself will need careful management to avoid a run-a-way and great care especially if the train has to go into a loop to allow a faster moving train to overtake it. As the train consists of coal empties from Fazackerley sidings to Crofton Colliery near Wakefield, the braking power of the engine will be critical as, apart from the guard's van, this is all there is. Heading the train is 'Austerity' 2-8-0 No.90333 built by the NBL Co. in July 1944 as No.70857.   *Allan Heyes*

Above: Rainford Junction, 1956. Although planned by the Liverpool and Bury Railway, it was opened by the L&Y on 20 November, 1848. Ten years later it closed to reopen a quarter of a mile east, the current station. This view of the 'Junction' is from the footbridge looking towards Liverpool, and shows the Ormskirk branch from the north, on the right, and the line off south to St. Helens, on the left. The bridge in the distance, partly obscured by the signal box, carries the route from Randle Junction on the St. Helens line to Bushy Lane Junction on the Ormskirk line. This enabled trains from the local pits to get to St. Helens. and then to Widnes and Garston's docks without traversing Rainford Junction. The platforms were of such length that passengers could transfer between main and branch trains by simply walking along the platform. Now, the line to Kirkby is single, and so a token is passed from engine crew to signalman.

Signalling Record Society, Scrimgeour collection

Left: Rainford Junction, 1956. This was the scene on a rainy 28 August at 9.42am. The train is the 9.13am SX from Liverpool Exchange to Bolton. It will draw up along the platform so that coaches are all accessible. While the potential for exchanges at the station were great, it must be remembered that the concept of regular, integrated, services was still in the future. When services over the branches stopped to the majority of stations in 1952, the standard, post-war service consisted of trains only at peak periods.

J. Peden collection

Above: Rainford-Ormskirk 'Bob'. 'Bob' was the colloquial name given to small motor coaches like this. Several radiated out from Ormskirk, to Southport, Town Green and to Rainford. As the halts along the lines had rudimentary facilities, a set of steps was attached to the middle door which were capable of being let down. Note the L&Y name and crest on the sides. The destination board on No.5's coach reads 'Ormskirk, Rainford Junction & St. Helens'. A complicated chain and pulley system installed along the coach's roof enabled the driver to operate the regulator handle from the end compartment when running coach first. Basically, this was mechanically unsound and so a bell system and code between the footplate and driver's compartment was used. Another method used was the tried and tested verbal one! When newly built by Hughes, engine and coach both had the same number. However, maintainance of the engines took place at Horwich and of the coaches at Newton Heath. This resulted in good units being out of action due to the 'other half' being repaired. Subsequently, it was rare to find engines and coaches bearing the same numbers. This style of service lasted from 1906 until the 1930s when Aspinall 2-4-2T auto fitted trains took over. Engine No.5 became LMS No.10602 and was involved in an accident in Yorkshire, at Crofton South Junction on 30 November 1926. A brake hanger fractured, ramping the unit from the rails. A passing freight train ran into the engine: it was withdrawn in June the next year. *J. Peden collection*

Below: Rainford Junction, 1902. Probably the most numerous wheel arrangement around the turn of the century was 0-6-0 for tender locos., illustrating the vast amounts of unfitted freight carried. On 14 August, Aspinall loco. No.1054 brings a freight from Liverpool across the line from Ormskirk, on the right. This engine became LMS No.12096 before withdrawal at the start of 1934. Not only does the signal box have a different roof and steps, there are several signals that were cut down to size by the time the 1956 view was taken. *LCGB, Ken Nunn collection*

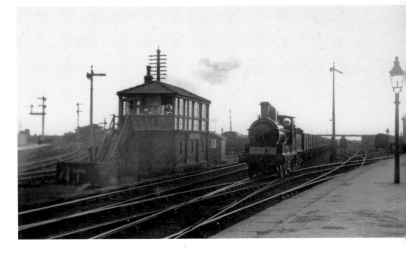

STATION ACCOMMODATION.						CRANE POWER. Tons Cwts.	STATIONS, &c.	COUNTY.	COMPANY.	POSITION.
G	.	F	L	H	C	10 0	**WIGAN—** (Station)	Lancs	L. N. E. (G. C.)...............	Hindley and Wigan (Central).
.	.	.	.	.	.	. .	Almond, J. B., Standish Brewery	Lancs	L. M. S. (L. N. W.)	Rylands & Son's Gidlow Works.
							Bickershaw Collieries—			
.	.	.	.	.	.	. .	Abram Colliery, North ...	Lancs	L. M. S. (L. N. W.)	Pennington and Platt Bridge.
.	.	.	.	.	.	. .	Abram Colliery, South ...	Lancs	L. M. S. (L. N. W.)	Pennington and Platt Bridge.
.	.	.	.	.	.	. .	Bickershaw or Plank Lane Colliery......................	Lancs	L. M. S. (L. N. W.)	Pennington and Platt Bridge.
.	.	.	.	.	.	. .	Brindley, Eli	Lancs	L. M. S. (L. N. W.)	{ Wigan Coal Corpn., Ltd., Bamfurlong Colliery. } Wigan Coal Corpn., Ltd., Mains Colliery.
.	.	.	.	.	.	. .	Bryn Hall Colliery Co.'s Sid.	Lancs	L. M. S. (L. N. W.)	Wigan and Bryn.
.	.	.	.	.	.	. .	**Burnett & Co.'s Siding**	Lancs	L. M. S. (L. N. W.)	Springs Branch.
.	.	.	.	.	.	. .	Canal Siding	Lancs	L. M. S. (L. & Y.)............	Wigan.
.	P	F	.	H	C	. .	Central	Lancs	L. N. E. (G. C.)...............	Terminus.
							Central Wagon Co.—			
.	.	.	.	.	.	. .	Gravel Hole Siding........	Lancs	L. M. S. (L. N. W.)	Springs Branch.
.	.	.	.	.	.	. .	Ince Hall Middle Place Sid.	Lancs	L. M. S. (L. N. W.)	Springs Branch.
.	.	.	.	.	.	. .	Chorley Wagons, Ltd..........	Lancs	L. M. S. (L. N. W.)	Crompton & Shawcross' Fir Tree House Colliery.
.	.	.	.	.	.	. .	Clare & Co.'s Siding	Lancs	L. M. S. (L. N. W.)	Pemberton Branch.
.	.	.	.	.	.	. .	Crompton & Shawcross Fir Tree House Colliery ...	Lancs	L. M. S. (L. N. W.)	Wigan and Platt Bridge.
.	.	.	.	.	.	. .	Garswood Brick & Tile Co., Ltd.	Lancs	L. M. S. (L. N. W.)	Garswood Hall Colliery.
.	.	.	.	.	.	. .	Garswood Hall Collieries, Ltd., Long Lane Colliery	Lancs	L. M. S. (L. N. W.)	Bamfurlong and Golborne.
.	.	.	.	.	.	. .	Garswood Hall Colliery	Lancs	L. M. S. (L. N. W.)	Wigan and Bryn.
.	.	.	.	.	.	. .	Hodgson & Co.	Lancs	L. M. S. (L. N. W.).........	Crompton & Shawcross Fir Tree House Colliery.
.	.	.	.	.	.	. .	Ince Wagon & Ironworks ...	Lancs	{ L. M. S. (L. N. W.) ...... } { L. N. E. (G. C.)............ }	Springs Branch. Lower Ince.
.	.	.	.	.	.	. .	Lancashire & Yorkshire Waggon Co., Ltd.	Lancs	L. M. S. (L. N. W.).........	Bickershaw Cols. Abram Col. North.
							Lancashire Steel Corporation, Ltd.—			
.	.	.	.	.	.	. .	Artificial Stone Works, Hindley Road Siding...	Lancs	L. M. S. (L. N. W.)	Springs Branch.
.	.	.	.	.	.	. .	Hindley Road Iron & Steel Works & Coke Ovens	Lancs	L. M. S. (L. N. W.).........	Springs Branch.
.	.	.	.	.	.	. .	Rose Bridge Iron & Steel Works	Lancs	L. M. S. (L. N. W.).........	Haigh Junc. and De Trafford Junc.
.	.	.	.	.	.	. .	Round House Iron Works	Lancs	L. M. S. (L. N. W.).........	Haigh Junc. and Rose Bridge Junc.
							L. M. & S. Rly. Co.— Carriage & Wagon Dept.			
.	.	.	.	.	.	. .	Siding	Lancs	L. M. S. (L. & Y.)	Wallgate.
.	.	.	.	.	.	. .	Locomotive Siding	Lancs	L. M. S. (L. & Y.)	Wallgate.
							Permanent Way Dept.—			
.	.	.	.	.	.	. .	Siding	Lancs	L. M. S. (L. & Y.)	Wallgate.
.	.	.	.	.	.	. .	Siding	Lancs	L. M. S. (L. N. W.)	Wigan.
.	.	.	.	.	.	. .	Siding	Lancs	L. M. S. (L. N. W.)	Springs Branch.
.	.	.	.	.	.	. .	Signal & Telegraph Siding	Lancs	L. M. S. (L. & Y.)	Wallgate.
.	.	.	.	.	.	. .	Timber Dept. (Garston)...	Lancs	L. M. S. (L. N. W.)	Wigan.
.	.	.	.	.	.	. .	Melling Bros.' Ince Forge Co.'s Siding............	Lancs	L. M. S. (L. N. W.)	Springs Branch.
.	.	.	.	.	.	. .	Monks Hall & Co.'s Church Iron Works	Lancs	L. M. S. (L. N. W.)	Springs Branch.
G	P	F	L	H	C	10 0	North Western	Lancs	L. M. S. (L. N. W.)	Preston and Warrington.
.	.	.	.	.	.	. .	Pemberton Col. Co. (1929), Ltd., Pemberton Cols. ...	Lancs	L. M. S. (L. N. W.)	Pemberton Branch.
.	.	.	.	.	.	. .	Rock Shale Construction Co., Ltd., Siding..........	Lancs	L. M. S. (L. N. W.).........	Pennington and Platt Bridge.
.	.	.	.	.	.	. .	Rose Bridge Col., Ltd., Rose Bridge Col.	Lancs	L. M. S. (L. N. W.)	Springs Branch.
.	.	.	.	.	.	. .	Round House Branch	Lancs	L. M. S. (L. N. W.)	Hindley & Amberswood & Red Rock.

This spread shows an extract from the *Railway Clearing House Official Handbook of Railway Stations*, in use in 1938, detailing the entries for Wigan.

STATION ACCOMMODATION.						CRANE POWER. Tons Cwts.		STATIONS, &c.	COUNTY.	COMPANY.	POSITION.
.	.	.	.	.	.	.	.	Rylands & Son's Gidlow Works	Lancs	L. M. S. (L. N. W.)	Wigan and Boars Head.
								Thompson & Co.'s Siding ...	Lancs	L. M. S. (L. N. W.)	Springs Branch.
G	P	F	L	H	C	10	0	Wallgate	Lancs	L. M. S. (L. & Y.).............	Liverpool and Bolton.
.	.	.	.	.	.	.	.	West Lancashire Brick Co.'s Siding	Lancs	L. M. S. (L. N. W.)	Pemberton Col. Co. (1929), Ltd., Pemberton Cols.
								West Leigh Coal Co.—			
.	.	.	.	.	.	.	.	Diggles North Siding ...	Lancs	L. M. S. (L. N. W.)	Hindley Green and Platt Bridge.
.	.	.	.	.	.	.	.	Diggles South Siding ...	Lancs	L. M. S. (L. N. W.)	Pennington and Platt Bridge.
								Wigan Coal Corpn., Ltd.—			
.	.	.	.	.	.	.	.	Almond Brook Sale Yard	Lancs	L. M. S. (L. N. W.).........	Gidlow Lane Colliery (Rylands Sid.)
.	.	.	.	.	.	.	.	Arley Siding	Lancs	L. M. S. (L. N. W.)	Wigan and Bamfurlong.
.	.	.	.	.	.	.	.	Bamfurlong Colliery	Lancs	L. M. S. (L. N. W.)	Wigan and Bamfurlong.
.	.	.	.	.	.	.	.	Belle Green Sale Yards (L. M. S.)	Lancs	L.M.S. (LNW)–LNE (GC)	Kirkless Hall Colliery.
.	.	.	.	.	.	.	.	Black Horse Siding	Lancs	L. M. S. (L. N. W.)	Gidlow Lane Col. (Rylands Siding).
.	.	.	.	.	.	.	.	California Roads (L.M.S.)	Lancs	L.M.S. (LNW)–LNE (GC)	Kirkless Hall Colliery.
.	.	.	.	.	.	.	.	Crawford Pit (L. M. S.)...	Lancs	L.M.S. (LNW)–LNE (GC)	Springs Branch.
.	.	.	.	.	.	.	.	Crook Canal Tip (L. M. S.)	Lancs	L.M.S. (LNW)–LNE (GC)	Gidlow Lane Colliery (Rylands Sid.)
.	.	.	.	.	.	.	.	Crook Sale Yard (L. M. S.)	Lancs	L.M.S. (LNW)–LNE (GC)	Gidlow Lane Colliery (Rylands Sid.)
.	.	.	.	.	.	.	.	Giants Hall Col. (L. M. S.)	Lancs	L.M.S. (LNW)–LNE (GC)	Gidlow Lane Col. (Rylands Siding).
.	.	.	.	.	.	.	.	Gidlow Lane Col. (Rylands Siding) (L. M. S.)	Lancs	L.M.S. (LNW)–LNE (GC)	Wigan and Standish.
.	.	.	.	.	.	.	.	Gidlow Lane Sale Yard (L. M. S.).................	Lancs	L.M.S. (LNW)–LNE (GC)	Gidlow Lane Colliery (Rylands Sid.)
.	.	.	.	.	.	.	.	Gidlow Saw Mill (L. M. S.)	Lancs	L.M.S. (LNW)–LNE (GC)	Gidlow Lane Colliery (Rylands Sid.)
.	.	.	.	.	.	.	.	Haigh Saw Mills Foundry (L. M. S.).................	Lancs	L.M.S. (LNW)–LNE (GC)	Haigh Saw Mills Sale Yard.
.	.	.	.	.	.	.	.	Haigh Saw Mills Sale Yard (L.M.S.)...........	Lancs	L.M.S. (LNW)–LNE (GC)	Springs Branch.
.	.	.	.	.	.	.	.	Haigh Saw Mills Workshops (L. M. S.)	Lancs	L.M.S. (LNW)–LNE (GC)	Haigh Saw Mills Sale Yard.
.	.	.	.	.	.	.	.	Ince Moss Colliery.........	Lancs	L. M. S. (L. N. W.)	Wigan and Bryn.
.	.	.	.	.	.	.	.	Ince Sale Yard	Lancs	L. M. S. (L. N. W.)	Arley Siding.
.	.	.	.	.	.	.	.	John Pit (L. M. S.)	Lancs	L.M.S. (LNW)–LNE (GC)	Gidlow Lane Col. (Rylands Siding).
.	.	.	.	.	.	.	.	Kirkless Hall Colliery (L. M. S.).................	Lancs	L.M.S. (LNW)–LNE (GC)	Springs Branch.
.	.	.	.	.	.	.	.	Kirkless Stores (L. M. S.)	Lancs	L.M.S. (LNW)–LNE (GC)	Kirkless Hall Colliery.
.	.	.	.	.	.	.	.	Kirkless Workshops	Lancs	L. M. S. (L. N. W.).........	Kirkless Hall Colliery.
.	.	.	.	.	.	.	.	Lindsay Siding (L. M. S.)	Lancs	L.M.S. (LNW)–LNE (GC)	Standish and Hindley.
.	.	.	.	.	.	.	.	Mains Colliery..............	Lancs	L. M. S. (L. N. W.).........	Bamfurlong and Golborne.
.	.	.	.	.	.	.	.	Maypole Colliery............	Lancs	L. M. S. (L. N. W.)	Moss Hall South Siding.
.	.	.	.	.	.	.	.	Meadow Pit Sale Yard (L. M. S.).................	Lancs	L.M.S. (LNW)–LNE (GC)	Kirkless Hall Colliery.
.	.	.	.	.	.	.	.	Moor No. 5 Pit Sale Yard (L. M. S.)	Lancs	L.M.S. (LNW)–LNE (GC)	Kirkless Hall Colliery.
.	.	.	.	.	.	.	.	Moss Collieries	Lancs	L. M. S. (L. N. W.).........	Ince Moss Colliery.
.	.	.	.	.	.	.	.	Moss Collieries	Lancs	L. M. S. (L. N. W.).........	Wigan and Bamfurlong.
.	.	.	.	.	.	.	.	Moss Hall Colliery	Lancs	L. M. S. (L. N. W.).........	Moss Hall South Siding.
.	.	.	.	.	.	.	.	Moss Hall South Siding...	Lancs	L. M. S. (L. N. W.).........	Platt Bridge and Hindley Green.
.	.	.	.	.	.	.	.	Moss Workshops............	Lancs	L. M. S. (L. N. W.).........	{ Ince Moss Colliery. Wigan and Bamfurlong.
.	.	.	.	.	.	.	.	Prospect Sale Yard (LMS)	Lancs	L.M.S. (LNW)–LNE (GC)	Gidlow Lane Col. (Rylands Siding).
.	.	.	.	.	.	.	.	Rawcliffe Sidings	Lancs	L. M. S. (L. N. W.).........	Kirkless Hall Colliery.
.	.	.	.	.	.	.	.	Robin Hill Pit..............	Lancs	L. M. S. (L. N. W.).........	Gidlow Lane Colliery (Rylands Sid.).
.	.	.	.	.	.	.	.	Standish Council Yard ...	Lancs	L. M. S. (L. N. W.).........	Gidlow Lane Colliery (Rylands Sid.).
.	.	.	.	.	.	.	.	Standish Slack Washery	Lancs	L. M. S. (L. N. W.).........	Gidlow Lane Colliery (Rylands Sid.).
.	.	.	.	.	.	.	.	Taylor Pit (L. M. S.)......	Lancs	L.M.S. (LNW)–LNE (GC)	Gidlow Lane Col. (Rylands Siding).
.	.	.	.	.	.	.	.	Victoria Col. (L. M. S.) ...	Lancs	L.M.S. (LNW)–LNE (GC)	Boars Head and Standish.
.	.	.	.	.	.	.	.	Wash Pit (L. M. S.)	Lancs	L.M.S. (LNW)–LNE (GC)	Springs Branch.
.	.	.	.	.	.	.	.	Wigan Junction Colliery & Brick Works	Lancs	L. M. S. (L. N. W.).........	Moss Hall South Siding.
.	.	.	.	.	.	.	.	Wigan Corporation Gas Works	Lancs	L. M. S. (L. & Y.)............	Wigan.
.	.	.	.	.	.	.	.	Wigan Wagon Co.'s Works	Lancs	L. M. S. (L. N. W.)	Springs Branch.
.	.	.	.	.	.	.	.	Wood, J., & Sons, Ltd., Barley Brook Siding......	Lancs	L. M. S. (L. & Y.).........	Wigan and Gathurst.

Key: G – Goods Station.
P – Passenger and Parcel Station.
F – Furniture Vans, Carriages, Motor Cars, Portable Engines, and Machines on Wheels.
L – Livestock
H – Horse Boxes and Prize Cattle Vans
C – Carriages and Motor Cars by Passenger Train.

More steam memories around Wigan...

Above: Standish, 1954. Racing north, putting up plenty of smoke indicating hard work by the fireman, is a special train on May Day. 'Jubilee' class 4-6-0 N0.45603 *Solomon Islands* is passing Victoria Colliery; the tall signals in the background illustrate the desire to give the drivers as much advance warning of the line's condition as possible. *Ray Hinton*

Below: Springs Branch, 1956. 'Royal Scot' class 4-6-0 No.46170 *British Legion* pulls a 13-coach Barrow to Euston express in September. The engine shed, on the right, and No.1 box, on the left, make up the frame for the picture. *RAS*

Bickershaw Colliery, 1978. Several of the NCB's fleet of 'Austerity' 0-6-0STs were stationed here and saw active service almost to the closure of the colliery. Hence it became a mecca for steam enthusiasts after the demise of the main line engines. Storming away from the screens, up the bank to the exchange sidings is once-green-liveried engine No.7 with a train load of HAAs. One can almost hear the exhaust, sense the power and smell the engine as it powers its way up the gradient. During the 1984/5 miners strike, bunkers were installed to load the coal into 36T hoppers as part of a merry-go-round train to supply coal to Fiddlers Ferry power station near Widnes.

Brian Dobbs

ACKNOWLEDGEMENTS

This book is meant to complement the comprehensively researched two-volume work *The Industrial Railways of the Wigan Coalfield* by Townley, Smith and Peden.

The author wishes to express a great deal of thanks to Ray Farrell and Allan Heyes for granting access to their extensive photographic collections.

Other photographs have come from:
M Christensen, JA Peden, PB Booth/ Neville Stead collection, RS Carpenter, B Hoper incorporating the AK Jones collection, GB Ellis, Norman Preedy archive, A Vaughan collection, John Ryan collection, Stations UK, RAS Marketing, Peter Hutchinson, CHA Townley, MA King, Bernard Matthews collection, IG Holt, Eddie Bellass, HF Wheller, FW Shuttleworth, RK Blencowe, B Lord, RCTS including ND Mundy, HC Casserley, L Hanson, John Marshall, Robert Humm collection, AJ Sommerfield, Mowat collection, Graham Earl, Ken Nunn (LCGB), J Cooper-Smith, D Ibbotson, B Barlow, Brian Dobbs, Ray Hinton.

The following societies have been most helpful:
Historical Model Railway Society, Great Central Railway Society, Lancashire & Yorkshire Railway Society, Signalling Record Society, Scrimgeour collection, Industrial Railway Society, London & North Western Railway Society.

Local studies libraries and their staff in the area have been of great help, as well as the Lancashire PRO at Preston.

This volume is dedicated to the residents of Wigan, who, by their encouragement and hospitality made it possible: I thank you.

The Industrial Railways of the Wigan Coalfield
Part 1 – West and South of Wigan

by CHA Townley, FD Smith, JA Peden

There were over 200 collieries and associated industrial concerns around Wigan at the beginning of the twentieth century, serviced by a large network of railways and canals.

This book reviews the development of rail and canal transport in and around Wigan from the eighteenth century to the present day, and provides a breif history of the collieries and other major industries of the Wigan coalfield. It contains much original material, not previously published, research by the authors in local newspapers, county records, railway archives and from discussions with former employees in the coalfield.

The private railway systems operated by the colliery companies and other establishments are described in detail, as are the locomotives employed on them.

Contents of this volume:

Introduction; Development of the canal and railway system, including a railway chronology; Orrell and Norley Hall; Pemberton; Winstanley and Worsley Mesnes; The early Ince Collieries; Developments at Ince -1845 to 1900; Ince in the Twentieth Century; Pearson and Knowles Ince Collieries; Amberswood and Strangeways Hall; Platt Bridge, Bamfurlong and Mains; Low Hall, Maypole and Wigan Junction; Edge Green, Brynn and Garswood; Skelmersdale and Bickerstaffe; Rainford, Upholland and Orrell.

The text is complemented by tables of locomotives, references, 30 specially drawn large scale maps and 45 black and white photographs.

272 pages, Hardback, 247 x 176 mm, £20.00
ISBN 1 870754 18 2

The Industrial Railways of the Wigan Coalfield
Part 2 – North and East of Wigan

by CHA Townley, FD Smith, JA Peden

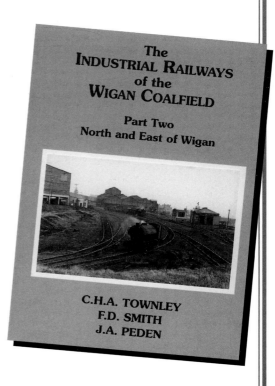

This volume completes the history of industrial railways around Wigan. Apart from comprehensive details of collieries, the book has much of interest to locomotive enthusiasts, with the story of the fascinating variety of locomotives and railcars built in the vicinity. It covers the following areas and undertakings:

Haigh and Aspull; Kirkless; the Wigan Coal and Iron Co. Ltd. and the Wigan Coal Corporation Ltd.; Shevington, Appley Bridge and Gathurst; From Douglas Bank to Westwood; North of Wigan; Standish; Coppull; Chorley and Adlington; Blackrod and Westhoughton; Westleigh; Bickershaw and Hindley Green; The Locomotives of the Wigan Coal and Iron Co. Ltd. and the Wigan Coal Corporation Ltd.; Locomotives built by Walker Brothers and Atkinson Walker; Locomotives built at the Haigh Foundry; Locomotive Dealers in Wigan; The Steam Ships of the Wigan Coal and Iron Company.

The text is complemented by tables of locomotives, references, 26 specially drawn maps and 55 black and white photographs.

Hardback, 247 x 176 mm, 260 pages, £19.95
ISBN 1 870754 23 9